ISA

Introduced by

SHEILA CASSIDY

DARTON · LONGMAN + TODD

This edition of the Book of Isaiah first published in 2010 by
Darton, Longman and Todd Ltd
1 Spencer Court
140-142 Wandsworth High Street
London SW18 4JJ

Nihil obstat Anthony Cowan
Imprimatur Rt Rev John Crowley V. G. Bishop in Central London
Westminster 4th September 1989

*The Nihil obstat and Imprimatur are a declaration that a book or pamphlet is
considered to be free from doctrinal or moral error. It is not implied that those who
have granted the Nihil obstat and Imprimatur agree with the contents, opinions or
statements expressed.*

ISBN 978-0-232-52833-6

A catalogue record for this book is available from the British Library.

Produced by Judy Linard
Printed and bound in Great Britain by Thomson Litho, East Kilbride,
Scotland

INTRODUCTION

Sheila Cassidy

The first thing I must say about the Prophet Isaiah is that his very name produces in me frissons of delight! My Jerusalem Bible tells me that he was a poet of genius, a fact I have no difficulty in believing.

It tells me, too, that he was a Mystic, as indeed were most of the prophets, and that explains it: the frissons, I mean. So when you think Isaiah, think Blake; think Hopkins, R.S. Thomas, Donne, Rumi, Hafiz and all the other great poets who were blessed with that marvellous yet terrifying closeness to the Divine.

My Jerusalem Bible introduction to the teaching of the prophets talks about what I like to call the 'Three Ms': Monotheism, Morality and Messianism. These three are the key theological themes of the Old Testament and explain, for me, why these books are crucial to my understanding of the all powerful God who is not only transcendent: beyond all knowing, but also, amazingly, immanent: as close to me as my own heart.

If Isaiah is new to you, or just a name you have heard in church, you might try reading my favourite passages and then move on to find your own.

I'd like to begin, not at the beginning of the book but with the man himself. Oh yes! He was real, a human person, like Jesus, like you, like me. Isaiah was born in 756BC: around two and a half thousand years ago. In 740BC, when he was only sixteen, he had a mind-blowing experience of the Divine: a vision of God surrounded by his angels:

> In the year of King Uzziah's death, I saw the Lord Yahweh seated on a high throne; his train filled the sanctuary; above him stood seraphs, each one with six wings: two to cover its face, two to cover its feet and two for flying. (Isaiah 6:1–3)

Spooky, isn't it? The angels cry out to each other:

> Holy, holy, holy is the Lord God,
> His glory fills the whole earth. (Isaiah 6:3)

The threshold shakes and the temple is filled with smoke and the young Isaiah is scared witless. Instantly he realises that he is 'unclean', sinful before the Lord, and God responds by sending a seraph to purify him by touching his mouth with a burning coal. There follows one of the most moving and timeless interactions in history: God says, 'Whom shall I send?' And Isaiah, his heart pounding, says his 'Yes', his 'I do'. Here we receive a glimpse of the amazing phenomenon of Divine call: something which continues to this day. Think Gladys Aylward, the London parlour maid who felt called to be a missionary in China, Joan of Arc, Abraham, Martin Luther King and Mother Teresa. Throughout history there runs a gold thread of witness: the lives of men and women who hear God's call and, shaking in their shoes, mutter, like Isaiah:

'Lord: Here I am, send me'. (Isaiah 6:8)

One of my favourite passages is the prophet's ranting against religious hypocrisy. You'll find it in chapter one. Try translating it into language for our own day:

'What are your endless sacrifices to me?' says Yahweh! (Isaiah 1:11)

The next stop off on your rapid journey through Isaiah is chapter nine: you've probably heard it more than once at some Christmas Carol Service. I love reading this passage:

The people that walked in darkness has seen a great light;
On those who live in a land of deep shadow

A light has shone. (Isaiah 9:1)

This is a prophecy of Hope: freedom to prisoners, an end to wars, a child born to the barren woman, a cure found for cancer. This isn't the material of fairy stories, false promises, magical cures. No, it is hope: the knowledge that God can, and will, turn darkness into light, bring good out of evil and life out of death.

This passage is an example of Messianic prophecy; Christians understand it as the foretelling of the birth of Jesus:

> For there is a child born for us,
> a son given us
> and dominion is laid on his shoulders;
> and this is the name they give him:
> Wonder-Counsellor, Mighty-God
> Eternal-Father, Prince-of-Peace. (Isaiah 9:5)

I find it fascinating that Jesus chose a reading from Isaiah to proclaim the nature of his mission. Move forward to Chapter 61:

> The Spirit of the Lord Yahweh has been given me,
> For Yahweh has anointed me.
> He has sent me to bring good news to the poor,
> to bind up hearts that are broken,

to proclaim liberty to captives,
freedom to those in prison. (Isaiah 61:1–2)

Think Gandhi, Mandela, William Wilberforce, Elizabeth
Fry, the Suffragettes and Albert Schweitzer: all men and
women called by God (not only our Christian God!) to
feed the hungry, clothe the naked, heal the sick and
comfort the grieving. The phenomenon of 'call' is alive
and well because God is alive and well:

Holy God, Holy and Strong,
Holy and Deathless,
Have mercy on us.
(Orthodox and Catholic Liturgies)

Last, but not least, let me introduce you to the amazing
Servant Songs. No matter that these are attributed to
one of Isaiah's followers, who lived two hundred years
after him:

Who could believe what we have heard,
and to whom has the power of Yahweh been
     revealed?
Like a sapling he grew up in front of us,
like a root in arid ground.
Without beauty, without majesty (we saw him),
no looks to attract our eyes;
a thing despised and rejected by men,

a man of sorrows and familiar with suffering,
a man to make people screen their faces;
he was despised and we took no account of him.
And yet ours were the sufferings he bore,
ours the sorrows he carried.
On him lies a punishment that brings us peace,
and through his wounds we are healed.
(Isaiah 53:1-5)

Is this passage purely messianic, I wonder? Is Isaiah foretelling Jesus' passion and death; the great act of Redemption which benefits us all? My guess is he is talking about Jesus but also about all who suffer, lay down their lives for their friends. I see not only the crucified Man of Sorrows but soldiers with their faces shot away, men and women, naked, tortured and bleeding; fire fighters burned in the act of rescue and mothers who starve so that their children may eat. This is powerful stuff. Read on!

ISAIAH

THE FIRST PART OF THE BOOK OF ISAIAH

Prophecies Before the Syro-Ephraimite War

TITLE

1 The vision of Isaiah son of Amoz concerning Judah and Jerusalem, which he received in the reigns of Uzziah, Jotham, Ahaz and Hezekiah kings of Judah.

AGAINST AN UNGRATEFUL PEOPLE

² Listen, you heavens; earth, attend,
  for Yahweh is speaking,
 'I have reared children
  and brought them up,
 but they have rebelled against me.

³ The ox knows its owner
    and the donkey its master's crib;
Israel does not know,
    my people do not understand.'

⁴ Disaster, sinful nation,
    people weighed down with guilt,
race of wrong-doers, perverted children!
They have abandoned Yahweh,
    despised the Holy One of Israel,
they have turned away from him.

⁵ Where shall I strike you next,
    if you persist in treason?
The whole head is sick,
    the whole heart is diseased,

⁶ from the sole of the foot to the head
    there is nothing healthy:
only wounds, bruises and open sores
not dressed, not bandaged,
    not soothed with ointment,

⁷ your country a desolation,
    your towns burnt down,
your soil, foreigners lay it waste
    before your eyes,
a desolation like devastation by foreigners.

⁸ The daughter of Zion is left
    like a shanty in a vineyard,
like a shed in a cucumber field,
    like a city besieged.

⁹ Had Yahweh Sabaoth not left us
        a few survivors,
    we should be like Sodom,
        we should be the same as Gomorrah.

AGAINST HYPOCRISY

¹⁰ Hear what Yahweh says,
        you rulers of Sodom;
    listen to what our God teaches,
        you people of Gomorrah.

¹¹ 'What are your endless sacrifices to me?'
        says Yahweh.
    'I am sick of burnt offerings of rams
    and the fat of calves.
    I take no pleasure in the blood
    of bulls and lambs and goats.
¹² When you come
        and present yourselves before me,
    who has asked you
        to trample through my courts?
¹³ Bring no more futile cereal offerings,
    the smoke from them fills me with disgust.
    New Moons, Sabbaths, assemblies—
        I cannot endure solemnity
            combined with guilt.
¹⁴ Your New Moons and your meetings

I utterly detest;
to me they are a burden
I am tired of bearing.
¹⁵ When you stretch out your hands
I turn my eyes away.
You may multiply your prayers,
I shall not be listening.
Your hands are covered in blood,
¹⁶ wash, make yourselves clean.
Take your wrong-doing out of my sight.
Cease doing evil. ¹⁷Learn to do good,
search for justice, discipline the violent,
be just to the orphan, plead for the widow.

¹⁸ 'Come, let us talk this over,' says Yahweh.
'Though your sins are like scarlet,
they shall be white as snow;
though they are red as crimson,
they shall be like wool.
¹⁹ If you are willing to obey,
you shall eat the good things of the earth.
²⁰ But if you refuse and rebel,
the sword shall eat you instead—
for Yahweh's mouth has spoken.'

LAMENT FOR JERUSALEM

²¹ The faithful city,
   what a harlot she has become!
   Zion, once full of fair judgement,
   where saving justice used to dwell,
   but now assassins!

²² Your silver has turned into dross,
   your wine is watered.
²³ Your princes are rebels,
   accomplices of brigands.

   All of them greedy for presents
   and eager for bribes,
   they show no justice to the orphan,
   and the widow's cause
      never reaches them.

²⁴ Hence, the Lord Yahweh Sabaoth,
   the Mighty One of Israel, says this,
   'Disaster, I shall get the better
      of my enemies,
   I shall avenge myself on my foes.

²⁵ 'I shall turn my hand against you,
   I shall purge your dross
      as though with potash,
   I shall remove all your alloy.

²⁶ 'And I shall restore your judges as at first,
    your counsellors as in bygone days,
    after which you will be called
        City of Saving Justice,
    Faithful City.'

²⁷ Zion will be redeemed by fair judgement,
    and those who return, by saving justice.
²⁸ Rebels and sinners alike will be destroyed,
    and those who abandon Yahweh
        will perish.

AGAINST SACRED TREES

²⁹ How ashamed you will be
        of the terebinths
    which gave you such delight;
    and how you will blush
        for the gardens which you chose!
³⁰ For you will be like a terebinth
        with faded leaves,
    like a garden without water;
³¹ the strong will become like tinder,
        his work like the spark;
    both will go up in flames together,
    with no one to put them out.

EVERLASTING PEACE

2 The vision of Isaiah son of Amoz, concerning Judah and Jerusalem.

² It will happen in the final days
   that the mountain of Yahweh's house
   will rise higher than the mountains
   and tower above the heights.
   Then all the nations will stream to it,
³ many peoples will come to it and say,

   'Come, let us go up
   to the mountain of Yahweh,
   to the house of the God of Jacob
   that he may teach us his ways
   so that we may walk in his paths.'
   For the Law will issue from Zion
   and the word of Yahweh from Jerusalem.

⁴ Then he will judge between the nations
   and arbitrate between many peoples.
   They will hammer their swords
      into ploughshares
   and their spears into sickles.
   Nation will not lift sword against nation,
   no longer will they learn how to make war.

⁵ House of Jacob, come,
let us walk in Yahweh's light.

THE BRILLIANCE OF YAHWEH'S MAJESTY

⁶ You have rejected your people,
the House of Jacob,
for it has long been full of sorcerers
like the Philistines,
and is overrun with foreigners.
⁷ The country is full of silver and gold
and treasures unlimited,
the country is full of horses,
its chariots are unlimited;
⁸ the country is full of idols.
They bow down
before the work of their hands,
before what their own fingers
have made.

⁹ Human nature has been humbled,
humankind brought low:
do not raise them again!
¹⁰ Go into the rock, hide in the dust,
in terror of Yahweh,
at the brilliance of his majesty,
when he arises to make the earth quake.

¹¹ Human pride will lower its eyes,
  human arrogance will be humbled,
  and Yahweh alone will be exalted,
      on that day.
¹² That will be a day for Yahweh Sabaoth,
  for all who are majestic and haughty,
  for all who are proud, to be brought low,
¹³ for all the cedars of Lebanon,
      high and proud,
  and for all the oaks of Bashan;
¹⁴ for all the high mountains
  and for all the proud hills;
¹⁵ for every lofty tower
  and for every towering wall;
¹⁶ for all the ships of Tarshish
  and for everything held precious.

¹⁷ Human pride will be humbled,
  human arrogance brought low,
  and Yahweh alone will be exalted,
      on that day.

¹⁸ When the idols all disappear,
¹⁹ they will go into the caverns of the rocks
  and into the fissures of the earth
  in terror of Yahweh,
      at the brilliance of his majesty,
  when he arises to make the earth quake.

²⁰ That day, people will fling to moles and bats the silver idols and golden idols which have been made for them to worship,

²¹ and go into the crevices of the rocks
and the clefts in the cliffs,
in terror of Yahweh,
    at the brilliance of his majesty,
when he arises to make the earth quake.

²² Have no more to do with humankind,
which has only the breath in its nostrils.
How much is this worth?

ANARCHY IN JERUSALEM

3 Now the Lord Yahweh Sabaoth
is about to deprive Jerusalem and Judah
of resources and provisions—
all reserves of food, all reserves of water—
² of hero, warrior, judge, prophet,
diviner, elder, ³captain, dignitary,
counsellor, architect, soothsayer.
⁴ 'I shall give them boys for princes,
raw lads to rule over them.'
⁵ People will be ill-treated by one another,
each by his neighbour;
the young will insult the aged,

and the low, the respected.

⁶ Yes, a man will catch hold of his brother
in their father's house, to say,
'You have a cloak, so you be leader,
and rule this heap of ruins.'

⁷ And, that day, the other will protest,
'I am no healer;
in my house there is neither food
nor clothing;
do not make me leader of the people.'

⁸ For Jerusalem has collapsed
and Judah has fallen,
because their words and deeds
affront Yahweh
and insult his glorious gaze.

⁹ Their complacency bears witness
against them,
they parade their sin like Sodom;
they do not conceal it,
all the worse for them,
for they have hatched their own downfall.

¹⁰ Say, 'Blessed the upright,
for he will feed on the fruit of his deeds;

¹¹ woe to the wicked, it will go ill with him,
for he will be treated
as his actions deserve.'

¹² O my people,
their oppressors pillage them

and extortioners rule over them!
O my people, your rulers mislead you
and efface the paths you ought to follow!
¹³ Yahweh has risen to accuse,
is standing to pass judgement
on the people.
¹⁴ Yahweh is about to try
the elders and the princes of his people,
'You are the ones
who have ravaged the vineyard,
the spoils of the poor are in your houses.
¹⁵ By what right do you crush my people
and grind the faces of the poor?'
says the Lord Yahweh Sabaoth.

THE WOMEN OF JERUSALEM

¹⁶Yahweh says:

Because Zion's daughters are proud
and walk with heads held high
and enticing eyes—
with mincing steps they go,
jingling the bangles on their feet—
¹⁷ the Lord will give Zion's daughters
scabby heads,
Yahweh will lay their foreheads bare.

¹⁸ That day the Lord will take away the ornamental chains, medallions, crescents, ¹⁹pendants, bracelets, trinkets, ²⁰diadems, ankle-chains, necklaces, scent bottles, amulets, ²¹finger-rings, nose-rings, ²²party dresses, cloaks, scarves, purses, ²³mirrors, linen clothes, turbans and mantillas.

²⁴ Then, instead of perfume, a stink;
    instead of belt, a rope,
    instead of hair elaborately dressed,
        a shaven scalp,
    instead of gorgeous clothes,
        sacking round the waist,
    and brand marks instead of beauty.

MISERY IN JERUSALEM

²⁵ Your men will fall by the sword,
    your warriors in battle,
²⁶ and her gates will moan and mourn;
    she will sit on the ground, deserted.

4 That day, seven women will catch hold of one man and say, 'We will eat our own food, and wear our own clothing, but just let us bear your name. Take our disgrace away.'

YAHWEH'S SEEDLING

[2] That day, Yahweh's seedling
    will turn to beauty and glory,
what the earth brings forth
    will turn to the pride and ornament
of Israel's survivors.
[3] Those who are left in Zion
    and remain in Jerusalem
will be called holy,
all those in Jerusalem
    noted down to live.
[4] When the Lord has washed away
the filth of Zion's daughters
and with the wind of judgement
    and the wind of burning cleansed
Jerusalem of the blood shed in her,
[5] Yahweh will create,
over every house on Mount Zion
and over those who assemble there,
a cloud by day,
and by night smoke
    with the brightness of a flaring fire.
For over all will be the Glory
    as canopy and tent
to give shade by day from the heat,
refuge and shelter from the storm
    and the rain.

THE SONG OF THE VINEYARD

5 Let me sing my beloved the song of my friend for his vineyard.

My beloved had a vineyard
on a fertile hillside.

2 He dug it, cleared it of stones,
and planted it with red grapes.
In the middle he built a tower,
he hewed a press there too.
He expected it to yield fine grapes:
wild grapes were all it yielded.

3 And now, citizens of Jerusalem
and people of Judah,
I ask you to judge between me
and my vineyard.

4 What more could I have done
for my vineyard
that I have not done?
Why, when I expected it
to yield fine grapes,
has it yielded wild ones?

5 Very well, I shall tell you
what I am going to do to my vineyard:
I shall take away its hedge,
for it to be grazed on,
and knock down its wall,

for it to be trampled on.
⁶ I shall let it go to waste, unpruned, undug,
overgrown by brambles
and thorn-bushes,
and I shall command the clouds
to rain no rain on it.
⁷ Now, the vineyard of Yahweh Sabaoth
is the House of Israel,
and the people of Judah
the plant he cherished.
He expected fair judgement,
but found injustice,
uprightness, but found cries of distress.

CURSES

⁸ Woe to those who add house to house
and join field to field
until there is nowhere left
and they are the sole inhabitants
of the country.
⁹ Yahweh Sabaoth has sworn this
in my hearing,
'Many houses will be brought to ruin,
great and fine ones left untenanted;
¹⁰ for ten acres of vineyard
will yield only one barrel,
and ten bushel of seed

will yield only one bushel.'

11 Woe to those who get up early
    to go after strong drink,
and stay up late at night
    inflamed with wine.
12 Nothing but harp and lyre,
tambourine and pipe,
and wine for their drinking bouts.

Never a thought for the works of Yahweh,
never a glance
    for what his hands have done.
13 That is why my people is in exile,
    for want of perception;
her dignitaries starving,
    her populace parched with thirst.
14 That is why Sheol opens wide its throat
and gapes with measureless jaw
and down go her noblemen and populace
and her loud revellers merry to the last!

15 Human nature has been humbled,
    humankind brought low,
and the eyes of the proud
    have been humbled.
16 Yahweh Sabaoth is the more respected
    for his judgement,

God the Holy One
  has displayed his holiness by his justice!
¹⁷ Now the lambs will graze
  in their old pastures,
and the fields laid waste by fat cattle
  will feed the kids.

¹⁸ Woe to those who drag guilt along
  by the reins of duplicity,
drag along sin as though with a cart rope;
¹⁹ to those who say,
  'Why doesn't he do his work quickly
so that we can see it;
why doesn't the Holy One
  of Israel's design
    hurry up and come true
so that we can experience it?'

²⁰ Woe to those who call what is bad, good,
and what is good, bad,
who substitute darkness for light
and light for darkness,
who substitute bitter for sweet
and sweet for bitter.

²¹ Woe to those who think themselves wise
and believe themselves enlightened.

²² Woe to those whose might lies
    in wine bibbing,
their heroism in mixing strong drinks,
²³ who acquit the guilty for a bribe
and deny justice to the upright.
²⁴ Yes, as the flame devours the stubble,
as the straw flares up and disappears,
their root will be like decay
and their shoot be carried off like dust,
for having rejected the law
    of Yahweh Sabaoth,
for having despised the word
    of the Holy One of Israel.

YAHWEH'S ANGER

²⁵ This is why Yahweh's anger
    has blazed out against his people;
and he has raised his hand against them
    to strike them;
why the mountains have shuddered
and why corpses are lying like dung
    in the streets.
After all this, his anger is not spent.
No, his hand is still raised!

YAHWEH SUMMONS THE INVADERS

²⁶ He hoists a signal for a distant nation,
   he whistles them up
        from the ends of the earth;
   and see how swift, how fleet they come!
²⁷ None of them tired,
        none of them stumbling,
   none of them asleep or drowsy,
   none of them with belt unfastened,
   none of them with broken sandal-strap.

²⁸ Their arrows are sharpened,
   their bows all strung,
   their horses' hoofs
        you would think were flint
   and their wheels, a whirlwind!

²⁹ Their roar is like that of a lioness,
   like fierce young lions they roar,
   growling they seize their prey
   and carry it off,
        with no one to prevent it,

³⁰ growling at it, that day,
   like the growling of the sea.
   Only look at the country:
   darkness and distress,

and the light turned to darkness
by the clouds.

The Book of Immanuel

THE CALL OF ISAIAH

6 In the year of King Uzziah's death I saw the Lord seated on a high and lofty throne; his train filled the sanctuary. ²Above him stood seraphs, each one with six wings: two to cover its face, two to cover its feet and two for flying; ³and they were shouting these words to each other:

'Holy, holy, holy is Yahweh Sabaoth.
His glory fills the whole earth.'

⁴ The door-posts shook at the sound of their shouting, and the Temple was full of smoke. ⁵Then I said:

'Woe is me! I am lost,
for I am a man of unclean lips
and I live among a people of unclean lips,
and my eyes have seen the King,
    Yahweh Sabaoth.'

⁶ Then one of the seraphs flew to me, holding in its hand

a live coal which it had taken from the altar with a pair of tongs. [7]With this it touched my mouth and said:

> 'Look, this has touched your lips,
> your guilt has been removed
> and your sin forgiven.'

[8] I then heard the voice of the Lord saying:
'Whom shall I send? Who will go for us?'
And I said, 'Here am I, send me.' [9]He said:

> 'Go, and say to this people,
> "Listen and listen, but never understand!
> Look and look, but never perceive!"
[10] Make this people's heart coarse,
> make their ears dull, shut their eyes tight,
> or they will use their eyes to see,
> use their ears to hear,
> use their heart to understand,
> and change their ways and be healed.'

[11]I then said, 'Until when, Lord?' He replied, 'Until towns are in ruins and deserted, houses untenanted and a great desolation reigns in the land, [12]and Yahweh has driven the people away and the country is totally abandoned. [13]And suppose one-tenth of them are left in it, that will be stripped again, like the terebinth, like the oak, cut back to the stock; their stock is a holy seed.'

ISAIAH INTERVENES

7 In the reign of Ahaz son of Jotham, son of Uzziah king of Judah, Razon king of Aram advanced on Jerusalem with Pekah son of Remaliah king of Israel, to attack it; but he was unable to attack it. ²The House of David was informed: 'Aram has halted in Ephraimite territory.' At this, his heart and his people's hearts shook like forest trees shaking in the wind.

³Yahweh then said to Isaiah, 'Go out with your son Shear-Jashub,⁴ and meet Ahaz at the end of the conduit of the upper pool, on the road to the Fuller's Field, ⁴and say to him, "Pay attention and keep calm. Do not be frightened or demoralised by these two smouldering sticks of firewood, by the fierce anger of Razon, Aram and the son of Remaliah, ⁵or because Aram, Ephraim and the son of Remaliah have been plotting against you and saying: ⁶Let us mount an attack on Judah, destroy it, force it onto our side and install the son of Tabeel there as king.

⁷ "Lord Yahweh says this:

This will not happen, it will never occur,
⁸ for the head of Aram is Damascus,
and the head of Damascus is Razon;
another sixty-five years,
and Ephraim will cease to be a people.
The head of Ephraim is Samaria,

and the head of Samaria
is the son of Remaliah.
If you will not take your stand on me
you will not stand firm." '

ISAIAH INTERVENES AGAIN

[10]Yahweh spoke to Ahaz again and said:

[11] Ask Yahweh your God for a sign,
either in the depths of Sheol
or in the heights above.

[12] But Ahaz said, 'I will not ask. I will not put Yahweh to
the test.'
[13] He then said:

Listen now, House of David:
are you not satisfied
with trying human patience
that you should try
my God's patience too?
[14] The Lord will give you a sign in any case:
It is this: the young woman is with child
and will give birth to a son
whom she will call Immanuel.
[15] On curds and honey will he feed
until he knows how to refuse the bad

and choose the good.
[16] Before the child knows
how to refuse the bad
and choose the good,
the lands whose two kings
are frightening you
will be deserted.

[17] Yahweh will bring times for you,
your people and your ancestral House,
such as have not been seen
since Ephraim broke away from Judah
(the king of Assyria).

PREDICTION OF AN INVASION

[18] When that day comes,
Yahweh will whistle up mosquitoes
from the distant streams of Egypt
and bees from the land of Assyria,
[19] and they will all come and settle
on the streams in the gullies,
in the holes in the rocks,
on all the thorn-bushes
and on all the water-points.
[20] That day the Lord will shave,
with a razor hired
from the other side of the River

(with the king of Assyria),
the head and the hair of the leg,
and take off the beard, too.

²¹ When that day comes, each man will raise
one heifer and two sheep,

²² and because of the abundant milk
they give
(on curds will he feed)
all who are left in the country
will feed on curds and honey.

²³ When that day comes,
wherever there used to be
a thousand vines
worth a thousand pieces of silver,
all will be brambles and thorn-bushes;

²⁴ to be ventured into
only with arrows and bow,
for the country will be nothing
but brambles and thorn-bushes.

²⁵ No more will you venture
on any hillside formerly under the hoe
for fear of the brambles and thorn-bushes;
it will be fit only for pasturing the cattle,
a tramping-ground for sheep.

THE BIRTH OF A SON TO ISAIAH

8 Yahweh said to me, 'Take a large tablet and on it with an ordinary stylus write, "Maher-Shalal-Hash-Baz". ²And take reliable witnesses, the priest Uriah and Zechariah son of Jeberechiah.'

³I then had intercourse with the prophetess, who then conceived and gave birth to a son.⁵Yahweh said to me, 'Call him Maher-Shalal-Hash-Baz, ⁴for before the child knows how to say "mother" or "father", the wealth of Damascus and the booty of Samaria will be carried away while the king of Assyria looks on.'

SHILOAH AND THE EUPHRATES

⁵Yahweh spoke to me again and said, ⁶"Since this people has rejected the waters of Shiloah which flow smoothly, and has trembled before Razon and the son of Remaliah, ⁷now, against it, the Lord will bring the mighty, swelling waters of the River (the king of Assyria and all his glory); the River will flood up all its channels and overflow all its banks; ⁸it will flow into Judah, flooding everything and passing on; it will reach right up to the neck, and the spreading of its wings will cover the whole extent of your country, Immanuel!

⁹ Realise this, peoples, and be afraid,
   listen, all members of far-off nations!

Arm yourselves yet be afraid!
Arm yourselves yet be afraid!
¹⁰ Devise plans as you may:
    they will come to nothing!
Make what pronouncements you like;
    it will not come about!
For God is with us!'

ISAIAH'S MISSION

¹¹ For this was how Yahweh spoke to me
    when his hand seized hold of me
and he taught me not to follow
    the path of this people, saying,
¹² 'Do not call conspiracy
    all that this people calls conspiracy;
do not dread what they dread,
    have no fear of that.
¹³ Yahweh Sabaoth is the one
    you will proclaim holy,
him you will dread, him you will fear.
¹⁴ He will be a sanctuary,
    a stumbling-stone,
a rock to trip up
    the two Houses of Israel;
a snare and a trap
    for the inhabitants of Jerusalem,
¹⁵ over which many of them will stumble,

  fall and be broken,
 be ensnared and made captive.
¹⁶ Bind up the testimony,
  seal the instruction
in the heart of my disciples.'
¹⁷ My trust is in Yahweh who hides his face
  from the House of Jacob;
 I put my hope in him.
¹⁸ Look, I and the children
  whom Yahweh has given me
shall become signs and portents in Israel
  on behalf of Yahweh Sabaoth
   who dwells on Mount Zion.
¹⁹ And should people say to you,
 'Go and consult ghosts and wizards
  that whisper and mutter'—
a people should certainly
  consult its gods
and the dead on behalf of the living!
²⁰ As regards instruction and testimony,
 without doubt this is how they will talk,
 and hence there will be
  no dawn for them.

WANDERING IN DARKNESS

²¹ Oppressed and starving
  he will wander the country;

and, once starving,
>he will become frenzied
and curse his king and his God;
>turning his gaze upward,
22 then down to earth,
>there will be only anguish,
gloom, the confusion of night,
>swirling darkness.
23 For is not everything dark as night
>for a country in distress?

DELIVERANCE

As the past humbled the land of Zebulun and the land of
Naphtali, so the future will glorify the Way of the Sea,
beyond the Jordan, the territory of the nations.

9 The people that walked in darkness
have seen a great light;
on the inhabitants of a country
>in shadow dark as death
light has blazed forth.
2 You have enlarged the nation,
>you have increased its joy;
they rejoice before you
>as people rejoice at harvest time,
as they exult
>when they are dividing the spoils.

³ For the yoke that weighed on it,
>> the bar across its shoulders,
> the rod of its oppressor,
> these you have broken
>> as on the day of Midian.

⁴ For all the footgear
>> clanking over the ground
> and all the clothing rolled in blood,
> will be burnt, will be food for the flames.

⁵ For a son has been born for us,
> a son has been given to us,
> and dominion has been laid
>> on his shoulders;
> and this is the name he has been given,
> 'Wonder-Counsellor, Mighty-God,
> Eternal-Father, Prince-of-Peace'
⁶ to extend his dominion
>> in boundless peace,
> over the throne of David
>> and over his kingdom
> to make it secure and sustain it
> in fair judgement and integrity.
> From this time onwards and for ever,
> the jealous love of Yahweh Sabaoth
>> will do this.

THE ORDEALS OF THE NORTHERN KINGDOM

⁷ The Lord has launched a word at Jacob
and it has fallen on Israel;
⁸ and the people will all soon know it,
Ephraim and the inhabitants of Samaria,
who say in the pride
of their arrogant hearts,
⁹ 'The bricks have fallen down
but we shall rebuild with dressed stone;
the sycamores have been felled
but we shall replace them with cedars.'
¹⁰ But, against them,
Yahweh has raised their foe Razon,
he has whipped up their enemies,
¹¹ Aram to the east, Philistines to the west,
to devour Israel with gaping jaws.
After all this, his anger is not spent.
No, his hand is still raised!

¹² But the people would not come back
to him who struck them,
they would not seek out Yahweh Sabaoth;
¹³ hence Yahweh has topped
and tailed Israel,
cutting off palm and reed in a single day.
¹⁴ (The 'top' is the elder and the man of rank;

the 'tail' is the prophet teaching lies.)

¹⁵ This people's leaders have led them astray,
and those who are led by them
are swallowed up.
¹⁶ Hence the Lord
will no longer take delight
in their young people,
or pity on their orphans and widows,
since all of them are godless and evil,
and everything they say is madness.
After all this, his anger is not spent.
No, his hand is still raised!

¹⁷ Yes, wickedness has been burning
like a fire,
devouring bramble and thorn-bush,
setting the forest thickets ablaze—
up they go in billowing smoke!
¹⁸ The country has been set on fire
by the fury of Yahweh Sabaoth,
and the people are like food for the flames.
No one spares a thought for his brother.
¹⁹ They have sliced to the right
and are still hungry,
they have eaten to the left
and are not satisfied;
each devours the flesh of his own arm.
²⁰ Manasseh devours Ephraim,

Ephraim Manasseh,
together they turn against Judah.
After all this, his anger is not spent.
No, his hand is still raised!

10 Woe to those
who enact unjust decrees,
who compose oppressive legislation
2   to deny justice to the weak
and to cheat the humblest of my people
of fair judgement,
to make widows their prey
and to rob the orphan.
3   What will you do
on the day of punishment,
when disaster comes from far away?
To whom will you run for help
and where will you leave your riches,
4   to avoid squatting among the captives
or falling among the slain?
After all this, his anger is not spent.
No, his hand is still raised!

AGAINST THE KING OF ASSYRIA

5   Woe to Assyria, rod of my anger,
the club in their hands is my fury!
6   I was sending him

    against a godless nation,
commissioning him
    against the people who enraged me,
to pillage and plunder at will
and trample on them
    like the mud in the streets.

7 But this was not his intention
nor did his heart plan it so,
for he dreamed
    of putting an end to them,
of liquidating nations without number!

8 For he thought,
    'Are not my officers all kings?

9 Is not Calno like Carchemish,
Hamath like Arpad,
Samaria like Damascus?

10 As my hand has found
    the kingdoms of the false gods,
where there were more images
    than in Jerusalem and Samaria,

11 as I have treated Samaria
    and her false gods
shall I not treat Jerusalem
    and her statues too?'

12 When the Lord has completed all his work on Mount Zion and in Jerusalem, he will punish the fruit of the king of Assyria's boastful heart and the insolence of his haughty looks.

¹³ For he thinks:

'By the strength of my own arm
 I have done this
and by my own wisdom:
 how intelligent I have been!
I have abolished the frontiers
 between peoples,
I have plundered their treasures,
like a hero, I have subjugated
 their inhabitants.
¹⁴ My hand has found,
 as though a bird's nest,
the riches of the peoples.
Like someone collecting deserted eggs,
I have collected the whole world
while no one has fluttered a wing
or opened a beak to squawk.'

¹⁵ Does the axe claim more credit
 than the man who wields it,
or the saw more strength
 than the man who handles it?
As though a staff controlled
 those who raise it,
or the club could raise
 what is not made of wood!
¹⁶ That is why Yahweh Sabaoth

is going to inflict
leanness on his stout men,
and beneath his glory
  kindle a fever burning like a fire.
¹⁷ The light of Israel will become a fire
and its Holy One a flame
burning and devouring
his thorn-bushes and brambles in a day.
¹⁸ He will consume his luxuriant forest
  and productive ground,
he will ravage body and soul:
it will be like a consumptive wasting away;
¹⁹ and what remain of the trees of his forest
will be so few
  that a child could write their number.

THE LITTLE REMNANT

²⁰ When that day comes,
the remnant of Israel
  and the survivors of the House of Jacob
will stop relying on the man
  who strikes them
and will truly rely on Yahweh,
the Holy One of Israel.
²¹ A remnant will return,
  the remnant of Jacob,
to the mighty God.

²² Israel, though your people
        are like the sand of the sea,
only a remnant of them will return:
a destruction has been decreed
which will make justice overflow,
²³ for, throughout the country,
the Lord Yahweh Sabaoth
        will enforce the destruction
            now decreed.

TRUST IN GOD

²⁴That is why the Lord Yahweh Sabaoth says this:

My people who live in Zion,
do not be afraid of Assyria!
He may strike you with the rod,
he may raise the club against you
(on the way from Egypt),
²⁵ but in a very short time
the retribution will come to an end,
and my anger will destroy them.
²⁶ Yahweh Sabaoth will brandish
        a whip at him
as he struck Midian at Oreb's Rock,
will brandish his rod at the Sea
as he raised it on the way from Egypt.
²⁷ When that day comes,

his burden will fall from your shoulder,
and his yoke from your neck,
and the yoke will be destroyed ...

THE INVASION

28 He has reached Aiath,
he has moved on to Migron,
he has left his baggage train
at Michmash.
29 They have passed through the defile,
they have bivouacked at Geba.
Ramah quaked, Gibeah of Saul has fled.
30 Cry your loudest, Bath-Gallim!
Pay attention, Laish!
Answer her, Anathoth!
31 Madmenah has run away,
the inhabitants of Gebim
have taken cover.
32 This very day, as he halts at Nob,
he will shake his fist at the mountain
of the daughter of Zion,
the hill of Jerusalem.
33 See how the Lord Yahweh Sabaoth
violently lops off the foliage!
The ones standing highest are cut down,
the proudest are laid low!
34 The forest thickets fall beneath the axe,

and the Lebanon falls
 to the blows of a Mighty One.

THE DESCENDANT OF DAVID

11 A shoot will spring
 from the stock of Jesse,
a new shoot will grow from his roots.
2 On him will rest the spirit of Yahweh,
 the spirit of wisdom and insight,
 the spirit of counsel and power,
 the spirit of knowledge
  and fear of Yahweh:
3 his inspiration will lie in fearing Yahweh.
 His judgement will not be
  by appearances,
 his verdict not given on hearsay.
4 He will judge the weak with integrity
 and give fair sentence
  for the humblest in the land.
 He will strike the country
  with the rod of his mouth
 and with the breath of his lips
  bring death to the wicked.

5 Uprightness will be
  the belt around his waist,
 and constancy the belt about his hips.

⁶ The wolf will live with the lamb,
the panther lie down with the kid,
calf, lion and fat-stock beast together,
with a little boy to lead them.

⁷ The cow and the bear will graze,
their young will lie down together.
The lion will eat hay like the ox.

⁸ The infant will play
over the den of the adder;
the baby will put his hand
into the viper's lair.

⁹ No hurt, no harm will be done
on all my holy mountain,
for the country will be full
of knowledge of Yahweh
as the waters cover the sea.

RETURN FROM THE DISPERSION

¹⁰ That day, the root of Jesse,
standing as a signal for the peoples,
will be sought out by the nations
and its home will be glorious.

¹¹ When that day comes,
the Lord will raise his hand
a second time
to ransom the remnant of his people,
those still left, from Assyria,

        from Egypt,
from Pathros, Cush and Elam,
from Shinar, Hamath
        and the islands of the Sea.

¹² He will hoist a signal for the nations
and assemble the outcasts of Israel;
he will gather the scattered people
        of Judah
from the four corners of the earth.

¹³ Then Ephraim's jealousy will cease
and Judah's enemies be suppressed;
Ephraim will no longer
        be jealous of Judah
nor Judah any longer hostile to Ephraim,

¹⁴ but together they will swoop
        on the Philistines' back, to the west,
and together pillage
        the people of the east.
Edom and Moab
        will be subject to their sway
and the Ammonites will obey them.

¹⁵ Then Yahweh will dry up
        the gulf of the Sea of Egypt,
he will raise his hand against the River
with the heat of his breath.
He will divide it into seven streams
for them to cross dry-shod.

¹⁶ And there will be a highway

for the remnant of his people
for those still left, from Assyria,
as there was for Israel
when he came out of Egypt.

PSALM

12 And, that day, you will say:

'I praise you, Yahweh,
    you have been angry with me
but your anger is now appeased
    and you have comforted me.
2 Look, he is the God of my salvation:
I shall have faith and not be afraid,
for Yahweh is my strength and my song,
he has been my salvation.'

3 Joyfully you will draw water
    from the springs of salvation
4 and, that day, you will say,
    'Praise Yahweh, invoke his name.
Proclaim his deeds to the people,
    declare his name sublime.
5 Sing of Yahweh,
        for his works are majestic,
    make them known throughout the world.
6 Cry and shout for joy,

you who live in Zion,
For the Holy One of Israel
is among you in his greatness.'

Proclamations About Foreign Nations

AGAINST BABYLON

13 Proclamation about Babylon, seen by Isaiah son of Amoz.

2 On a bare hill hoist a signal,
shout for them, beckon them
to come to the Nobles' Gate.

3 I have issued orders
to my sacred warriors,
I have summoned my heroes
to serve my anger,
my proud champions.

4 The noise of a great crowd
in the mountains,
like an immense people,
the tumultuous sound of kingdoms,
of nations mustering:
it is Yahweh Sabaoth
marshalling the troops for battle.

5 They come from a distant country,
    from the far horizons,
  Yahweh and the instruments of his fury
  to lay the whole country waste.

6 Howl! For the Day of Yahweh is near,
  coming like devastation from Shaddai.

7 This is why all hands fall limp,
  why all the men are losing heart;

8 they are panic-stricken,
  seized with pains and convulsions;
  they writhe like a woman in labour,
  they look at one another appalled,
  with feverish faces.

9 Look, the Day of Yahweh is coming,
  merciless, with wrath and burning anger,
  to reduce the country to a desert
  and root out the sinners from it.

10 For in the sky the stars and Orion
  will shed their light no longer,
  the sun will be dark when it rises,
  and the moon will no longer give its light.

11 I am going to punish the world
      for its wickedness
  and the wicked for their guilt,
  and put an end to the pride of the arrogant
  and humble the haughtiness of despots.

12 I shall make people scarcer than pure gold,
  human life scarcer than the gold of Ophir.

¹³ This is why I am going to shake
the heavens,
why the earth will reel on its foundations,
under the wrath of Yahweh Sabaoth,
the day when his anger ignites.
¹⁴ Then like a hunted gazelle,
like sheep that nobody gathers in,
everyone will head back to his people,
everyone will flee to his native land.
¹⁵ All those who are found will be stabbed,
all those captured will fall by the sword,
¹⁶ their babies dashed to pieces
before their eyes,
their houses plundered, their wives raped.
¹⁷ Look, against them
I am stirring up the Medes
who care nothing for silver,
who set no value by gold.
¹⁸ Bows will annihilate the young men,
they will have no pity
for the fruit of the womb,
or mercy in their eyes for children.
¹⁹ And Babylon, that pearl of kingdoms,
that splendid jewel of the Chaldaeans,
will, like Sodom and Gomorrah,
be overthrown by God.
²⁰ Never again will anyone live there
or reside there

for all generations to come.
Never again will the Arab
    pitch his tent there,
or the shepherds
    bring their flocks to rest.
21 But beasts of the desert
    will make their haunt there
and owls fill their houses,
there ostriches will settle their home,
there goats will dance.
22 Hyenas will howl in its towers,
jackals in its delightful palaces,
for its doom is about to come
and its days will not last long.

THE END OF THE EXILE

14 Yahweh will have pity on Jacob, he will choose Israel once more and resettle them on their native soil. Foreigners will join them, attaching themselves to the House of Jacob. 2 Peoples will take them and escort them home, and the House of Israel will take them as slaves, men and women on Yahweh's soil. They will enslave those who enslaved them and will master their oppressors.

THE DEATH OF THE KING OF BABYLON

³When that day comes, and Yahweh gives you rest from your suffering and torment and the grim servitude to which you have been subjected, ⁴you will recite this satire on the king of Babylon and say:

> 'How did the tyrant end?
> How did his arrogance end?
> 5 Yahweh has broken the staff
> of the wicked,
> the sceptre of rulers,
> 6 furiously lashing peoples
> with continual blows,
> angrily hammering nations,
> pursuing without respite.
> 7 The whole world is at rest and calm,
> shouts of joy resounding,
> 8 the cypresses, the cedars of Lebanon,
> rejoice aloud at your fate,
> "Now that you have been laid low,
> no one comes up to fell us."
>
> 9 'On your account, Sheol below
> is astir to greet your arrival.
> He has roused the ghosts to greet you,
> all the rulers of the world.
> He has made all the kings of the nations

get up from their thrones.

¹⁰ They will all greet you with the words,
"So, you too are now as weak as we are!
You, too, have become like us.

¹¹ Your pride has been flung down to Sheol
with the music of your lyres;
under you a mattress of maggots,
over you a blanket of worms.

¹² How did you come to fall
    from the heavens,
Daystar, son of Dawn?
How did you come
    to be thrown to the ground,
conqueror of nations?

¹³ You who used to think to yourself:
I shall scale the heavens;
higher than the stars of God
I shall set my throne.
I shall sit on the Mount of Assembly
far away to the north.

¹⁴ I shall climb high above the clouds,
I shall rival the Most High."

¹⁵ Now you have been flung down to Sheol,
into the depths of the abyss!

¹⁶ 'When they see you,
    they will scrutinise you
and consider what you have become,

"Is this the man
    who made the world tremble,
who overthrew kingdoms?
¹⁷ He made the world a desert,
he levelled cities
and never freed his prisoners to go home."
¹⁸ All other kings of nations, all of them,
lie honourably, each in his own tomb;
¹⁹ but you have been thrown away,
    unburied,
like a loathsome branch,
covered with heaps of the slain
    pierced by the sword
who fall on the rocks of the abyss
like trampled carrion.
²⁰ 'You will not rejoin them in the grave,
for you have brought your country to ruin
and destroyed your people.
The offspring of the wicked
leave no name behind them.
²¹ Make ready to slaughter his sons
for the guilt of their father!
Never again must they rise
    to conquer the world
and cover the face of the earth
    with their cities.

²²'I will rise against them, declares Yahweh Sabaoth, and deprive Babylon of name, remnant, offspring and posterity, declares Yahweh. ²³I shall turn it into the haunt of hedgehogs, a swamp. I shall sweep it with the broom of destruction, declares Yahweh Sabaoth.'

AGAINST ASSYRIA

²⁴ Yahweh Sabaoth has sworn it,
  'Yes, what I have planned will take place,
  what I have decided will be so:

²⁵ 'I shall break Assyria in my country,
  I shall trample on him on my mountains.
  Then his yoke will slip off them,
  his burden will slip from their shoulders.'

²⁶ This is the decision taken
    in defiance of the whole world;
  this, the hand outstretched
    in defiance of all nations.

²⁷ Once Yahweh Sabaoth has decided,
    who will stop him?
  Once he stretches out his hand,
    who can withdraw it?

AGAINST THE PHILISTINES

²⁸In the year Ahaz died came this proclamation:

²⁹ All Philistia, do not rejoice
    because the rod which used to beat you
        is now broken,
    for the serpent stock will produce a viper,
    its offspring will be a flying dragon.
³⁰ While the first-born of the poor are grazing
    and the destitute are resting in safety,
    I shall make your stock die of hunger
    and then slaughter what remains of you.
³¹ Howl, gate! Shriek, city!
    Totter, all Philistia!
    For a smoke is coming from the north,
    and there are no deserters
        in those battalions.
³² What reply will be given then
    to the messengers of that nation?—
    That Yahweh founded Zion
    and there the poor of his people
        will find refuge.

ON MOAB

15 Proclamation about Moab:

Laid waste in a night,

Ar–Moab lies silent;
Laid waste in a night,
Kir–Moab lies silent.

2 The daughter of Dibon has climbed
to the high places to weep;
on Nebo and in Medeba
Moab laments.

Every head shaven,
every beard cut off,
3 they wear sackcloth in their streets;
on their roofs and in their squares,
everyone is lamenting
and collapsing in tears.

4 Heshbon and Elealeh are crying out
in distress,
their voices can be heard as far as Jahaz.
That is why the warriors of Moab
are shivering,
his soul trembles at the sound.
5 His heart cries out in distress for Moab,
whose fugitives are already at Zoar,
nearly at Eglath-Shelishiyah.

They climb the slope of Luhith,
weeping as they go;

on the road to Horonaim
they utter heart-rending cries.

6 The Waters of Nimrim
have become a waste land,
the grass dried up,
   the plants withered away,
nothing green any more.

7 That is why they are carrying
what they could save of their stores
across the Ravine of the Willows.

8 For the cry for help re-echoes
round the territory of Moab;
their wailing, right to Eglaim,
to Beer-Elim, their wailing;

9 Dimon's waters are swollen with blood,
and I have worse in store for Dimon:
a lion for those of Moab who survive,
for those left on its soil.

THE MOABITES' PETITION

16 Send the lamb
to the ruler of the land,
from Sela by the desert,

to the mountain of the daughter of Zion,

2 for soon, like a fluttered bird,
  like nestlings cast out,
  will be the women of Moab
      at the fords of the Arnon.

3 Hold a council, make a decision.
  At noon spread your shadow
  as if it were night.
  Hide those who have been driven out,
  do not betray the fugitive,

4 let those who have been driven out of Moab
  come and live with you;
  be their refuge in the face of the devastator.
  Once the oppression is past,
  and the devastation has stopped
  and those now trampling on the country
      have gone away,

5 the throne will be made secure
      in faithful love,
  and on it will sit in constancy
      within the tent of David
  a judge seeking fair judgement
      and pursuing uprightness.

6 We have heard about Moab's pride,
  about how very proud it is,
  about its arrogance, its pride, its rage,
  its bravado, which will come to nothing!

MOAB'S LAMENT

7 And so Moab is wailing for Moab,
   wailing, every one of them.
   For the raisin cakes of Kir–Hareseth
   you mourn, stricken with grief.
8 For Heshbon's vineyards are withering,
   the vine of Sibmah
   whose red grapes used to overcome
   the overlords of the nations.
   It used to reach to Jazer,
   had wound its way into the desert,
   its shoots grew so numerous
   they spread across the sea.
9 And so I weep, as Jazer weeps,
   for the vine of Sibmah.
   I water you with my tears,
   Heshbon and Elealeh.
   For over your harvest and vintage
   the cheering has died away;
10 joy and gladness
   have vanished from the orchards.
   No more revelry in the vineyards,
   no more happy shouting;
   no more the treader treads wine
       in the presses,
   the cheering has ceased.
11 That is why my whole being

quivers like harp strings for Moab,
my very heart, for Kir-Heres.

12 Moab will be seen,
wearing itself out on the high places
and going to its temple to pray,
but it will accomplish nothing.

13Such was the word which Yahweh spoke about Moab in
the past. 14And now Yahweh has spoken in these terms,
'Within three years, as a hired worker reckons them, the
glory of Moab will be humbled, despite its teeming
population. It will be reduced to nothing, an insignificant
remnant.'

AGAINST DAMASCUS AND ISRAEL

17 Proclamation about Damascus:

Damascus will soon cease to be a city,
it will become a heap of ruins.

2 Its towns, abandoned for ever,
will be pastures for flocks;
there they will rest
with no one to disturb them.

3 Ephraim will be stripped of its defences
and Damascus of its sovereignty;
and the remnant of Aram will be treated
like the glory of the Israelites—

declares Yahweh Sabaoth.

4 When that day comes,
    Jacob's glory will diminish,
from being fat he will grow lean;
5 as when a reaper gathers in
    the standing corn,
harvesting the ears of corn with his arm,
or when they glean the ears
    in the Valley of Rephaim,
6 nothing will remain but pickings,
as when an olive tree is beaten;
two or three berries left
on the topmost bough,
four or five berries
on the branches of the tree—
declares Yahweh, God of Israel.

7That day, a man will look to his Creator and his eyes
will turn to the Holy One of Israel. 8He will no longer
look to altars, his own handiwork, or to what his own
fingers have made: the sacred poles and incense-altars.

9 That day, its cities of refuge
    will be abandoned
as were the woods and heaths
at the Israelites' advance:
there will be desolation.

¹⁰ Since you have forgotten
    the God of your salvation,
and failed to keep the Rock,
    your refuge, in mind,
you plant pleasure-gardens,
you sow exotic seeds;
¹¹ the day you plant them,
    you get them to sprout,
and, next morning,
    your seedlings are in flower;
but the harvest will vanish
    on the day of disease
and incurable pain.

¹² Disaster! The thunder of vast hordes,
a thunder like the thunder of the seas,
the roar of nations
    roaring like the roar of mighty floods,
¹³ of nations roaring like the roar of ocean!
He rebukes them and far away they flee,
driven like chaff on the mountains
    before the wind,
like an eddy of dust before the storm.
¹⁴ At evening all is terror,
by morning all have disappeared.
Such will be the lot
    of those who plunder us,
such, the fate of our despoilers.

AGAINST CUSH

18 Disaster! Land of the whirring locust
beyond the rivers of Cush,

2 who send ambassadors by sea,
in little reed-boats across the waters!
Go, swift messengers
to a nation tall and bronzed,
to a people feared far and near,
a mighty and masterful nation
whose country is criss-crossed with rivers.

3 All you who inhabit the world,
you who people the earth,
when the signal is hoisted
on the mountains,
you will see,
when the ram's-horn is sounded,
you will hear.

4 For this is what Yahweh has told me,
'I shall sit here quietly looking down,
like the burning heat in the daytime,
like a dewy mist in the heat of harvest.'

5 For, before the harvest,
once the flowering is over
and blossom turns into ripening grape,
the branches will be cut off
with pruning knives,
and the shoots taken off, cut away.

⁶ All has been abandoned
to the mountain birds of prey
and the wild animals:
the birds of prey will summer on them,
and all the wild animals winter on them.

⁷Then, an offering will be brought to Yahweh Sabaoth on behalf of a people tall and bronzed, on behalf of a people feared far and near, on behalf of a mighty and masterful nation whose country is criss-crossed with rivers: to the place where the name of Yahweh Sabaoth resides, Mount Zion.

AGAINST EGYPT

19 Proclamation about Egypt:
Look! Yahweh, riding a swift cloud,
is coming to Egypt.
The false gods of Egypt totter before him
and Egypt's heart quails within her.
² I shall stir up Egypt against Egypt,
they will fight one another,
brother against brother,
friend against friend,
city against city,
kingdom against kingdom.
³ Egypt's spirit will fail within her
and I shall confound her deliberations.

They will consult false gods and wizards,
ghosts and sorcerers.

4 And I shall hand Egypt over
to the clutches of a cruel master,
a ruthless king will rule them—
declares Yahweh Sabaoth.

5 The waters will ebb from the sea,
the river will dry up and run low,

6 the streams will become foul,
the rivers of Egypt sink and dry up.
Rush and reed will turn black,

7 the Nile-plants on the banks of the Nile;
all the vegetation of the Nile,
will wither, blow away and be no more.

8 The fishermen will groan,
it will be mourning
for all who cast hook in the Nile;
those who spread nets on the waters
will lose heart.

9 The workers of carded flax
and the weavers of white cloth
will be confounded,

10 the weavers dismayed,
all the workmen dejected.

11 Yes, the princes of Zoan are fools,
Pharaoh's wisest councillors
make up a stupid council.
How dare you say to Pharaoh,

'I am descended from sages,
   I am descended from bygone kings'?
12 Where are these sages of yours?
   Let them tell you, so that all may know,
   the plans Yahweh Sabaoth has made
   against Egypt!
13 The princes of Zoan are fools,
   the princes of Noph, self-deceivers,
   the top men of her provinces
   have led Egypt astray.
14 Yahweh has infused them
   with a giddy spirit;
   they have led Egypt astray
      in all she undertakes
   like a drunkard straying about
      as he vomits.
15 Nowadays no one does for Egypt
   what top and tail,
   palm and reed used to do.

THE CONVERSION OF EGYPT

16That day Egypt will be like women, trembling and
terrified at the threatening hand of Yahweh Sabaoth, when
he raises it against her. 17The land of Judah will become
Egypt's shame; whenever she is reminded of it, she will be
terrified, because of the plan which Yahweh Sabaoth has
laid against her. 18That day in Egypt there will be five towns

speaking the language of Canaan and pledging themselves to Yahweh Sabaoth; one of them will be called City of the Sun. ¹⁹That day there will be an altar dedicated to Yahweh in the centre of Egypt and, close to the frontier, a pillar dedicated to Yahweh, ²⁰and this will be a sign and a witness to Yahweh Sabaoth in Egypt. When they cry to Yahweh for help because of oppressors, he will send them a Saviour and leader to deliver them. ²¹Yahweh will reveal himself to Egypt, and the Egyptians will acknowledge Yahweh that day and will offer sacrifices and cereal offerings, and will make vows to Yahweh and perform them. ²²And if Yahweh strikes Egypt, having struck he will heal, and they will turn to Yahweh who will hear their prayers and heal them. ²³That day there will be a highway from Egypt to Assyria. Assyria will have access to Egypt and Egypt have access to Assyria. Egypt will serve with Assyria.

²⁴That day Israel will make a third with Egypt and Assyria, a blessing at the centre of the world, ²⁵and Yahweh Sabaoth will bless them in the words, 'Blessed be my people Egypt, Assyria my creation, and Israel my heritage.'

RELATING TO THE CAPTURE OF ASHDOD

20 The year the general-in-chief, sent by Sargon king of Assyria, came to Ashdod and stormed and captured it ²at that time Yahweh spoke through Isaiah son of Amoz and said, 'Go, undo the sackcloth round your waist and take the sandals off your feet.' And he did so, and walked about, naked and barefoot. ³Yahweh then said, 'As my servant Isaiah has been walking about naked and barefoot for the last three years as a sign and portent for Egypt and Cush, ⁴so the king of Assyria will lead the captives of Egypt and the exiles of Cush, young and old, naked and barefoot, their buttocks bared, to the shame of Egypt. ⁵Then they will be afraid and ashamed of Cush their hope and Egypt their pride, ⁶and the inhabitants of this coast will say on that day, "Look what has happened to our hope, to those to whom we fled for help, to escape from the king of Assyria. How are we going to escape?"'

THE FALL OF BABYLON

21 Proclamation about the coastal desert:

As whirlwinds sweeping over the Negeb,
he comes from the desert,
    from a fearsome country.
2   A harsh vision has been shown me,
'The traitor betrays
    and the despoiler despoils.
Advance, Elam, lay siege, Media!'
I have cut short all groaning.
3   This is why my loins are racked with pain,
why I am seized with pangs
    like the pangs of a woman in labour;

I am too distressed to hear,
    too afraid to look.
4 My heart is bewildered,
    dread overwhelms me,
the twilight I longed for
    has become my horror.
5 They lay the table, spread the cloth,
they eat, they drink.
Up, princes, grease the shield!

6 For this is what the Lord has told me,
'Go, post a look-out,
    let him report what he sees.
7 He will see cavalry, horsemen two by two,
men mounted on donkeys,
    men mounted on camels;
let him watch alertly,
    be very alert indeed!'
8 Then the look-out shouted,
'On the watchtower, Lord,
I stay all day
and at my post
I stand all night.
9 Now the cavalry is coming,
    horsemen two by two.'
He shouted again and said,
'Babylon has fallen, has fallen,
and all the images of her gods

he has shattered to the ground!'
¹⁰ You whom I have threshed,
grain of my threshing-floor,
what I have heard
from Yahweh Sabaoth, God of Israel,
I am telling you now.

ON EDOM

¹¹ Proclamation about Dumah:

From Seir, someone shouts to me,
'Watchman, what time of night?
Watchman, what time of night?'

¹² The watchman answers,
'Morning is coming, then night again.
If you want to ask, ask!
Come back! Come here!'

AGAINST THE ARABS

¹³ Proclamation about the wastelands:

In the thickets, on the wastelands,
you spend the night,
you caravans of Dedanites.
¹⁴ Bring water for the thirsty!

The inhabitants of Tema went
with bread to greet the fugitive.
¹⁵ For these have fled before the sword,
the naked sword and the bent bow,
the press of battle.

¹⁶For this is what the Lord has told me,
'In one year's time as a hired worker reckons it, all the
glory of Kedar will be finished ¹⁷and, of the valiant archers,
the Kedarites, hardly any will be left, for Yahweh, God of
Israel, has spoken.'

AGAINST REJOICING IN JERUSALEM

22 Prophecy on the Valley of Vision:

Now what is the matter with you
for you all to be up on the housetops,
² full of excitement, boisterous town,
joyful city?
Your slain have not fallen to the sword
nor died in battle.
³ Your leaders have all fled together,
captured without a bow between them,
all who could be found
have been captured at a blow,
far though they had fled.
⁴ That is why I said,

'Turn your eyes away from me,
let me weep bitterly;
do not try to comfort me
over the ruin of the daughter
of my people.'

5 For this is a day of rout,
panic and confusion,
the work of the Lord Yahweh Sabaoth
in the Valley of Vision.
The wall is sapped,
cries for help ring out to the mountains.
6 Elam has picked up his quiver,
with manned chariots and horsemen,
and Kir has bared his shield.
7 Your fairest valleys are full of chariots
and the horsemen take up positions
at the gates;
8 thus falls the defence of Judah.
That day you turned your gaze
to the weapons in the House of the Forest.
9 You saw how many breaches there were
in the City of David.
You collected the waters of the lower pool.
10 You surveyed the houses in Jerusalem
and pulled houses down
to strengthen the wall.
11 Between the two walls

you made a reservoir
for the waters of the old pool.
But you did not look
to the Creator of these things,
you did not look to the One
who fashioned them long ago.

¹² That day the Lord Yahweh Sabaoth
called on you
to weep and mourn,
to shave your heads, to put on sackcloth.
¹³ But instead there is joy and merriment,
killing of oxen, slaughtering of sheep,
eating of meat, drinking of wine,
'Let us eat and drink,
for tomorrow we shall be dead.'
¹⁴ Then Yahweh Sabaoth revealed this
to my ears,
'This guilt will never be forgiven you,
until you are dead,'
says the Lord Yahweh Sabaoth.

AGAINST SHEBNA

¹⁵ The Lord Yahweh Sabaoth says this:

Go and find that steward,
Shebna, the master of the palace:

¹⁶ 'What do you own here,
      who gave you the right
   for you to hew yourself a tomb here?'
   He is hewing himself a tomb,
   is digging a resting-place for himself
      in the rock.
¹⁷ But Yahweh will throw you away,
      strong as you are,
   will grasp you in his grip,
¹⁸ will screw you up into a ball,
   a ball thrown into a vast space.
   There you will die,
      with your splendid chariots,
   disgrace to your master's palace!
¹⁹ I shall hound you from your office,
   I shall snatch you from your post
²⁰ and, when that day comes,
   I shall summon my servant
   Eliakim son of Hilkiah.
²¹ I shall dress him in your tunic,
   I shall put your sash round his waist,
   I shall invest him with your authority;
   and he will be a father
   to the inhabitants of Jerusalem
   and to the House of Judah.
²² I shall place the key of David's palace
      on his shoulder;
   when he opens, no one will close,

when he closes, no one will open.
²³ I shall drive him like a nail
into a firm place;
and he will become a throne of glory
for his family.

²⁴'On him will depend all the glory of his family, the descendants and offspring, all the vessels of small capacity too, from cups to pitchers. ²⁵That day, declares Yahweh Sabaoth, the nail driven into a firm place will give way, will be torn out and fall. And the whole load hanging on it will be lost. For Yahweh has spoken.'

AGAINST TYRE

23 Proclamation about Tyre:

Howl, ships of Tarshish,
for all has been destroyed—
no more houses, no way of getting in:
the news has reached them from Kittim.
² Be struck dumb, inhabitants of the coast,
you merchants of Sidon,
whose messengers cross the sea
³ to the wide ocean.
The grain of the Canal,
the harvest of the Nile,
formed her revenue.

She was the market for the nations.

4 Blush, Sidon (citadel of the seas),
   for this is what the sea has said,
   'I have felt no birth-pangs,
        never given birth,
   never reared boys nor brought up girls.'

5 When the news reaches Egypt,
   they will tremble to hear Tyre's fate.
6 Cross to Tarshish, howl,
        inhabitants of the coast.

7 Is this your proud city
   founded far back in the past,
   whose steps led her far afield
   to found her colonies?
8 Who took this decision
   against Tyre,
        who used to hand out crowns,
   whose traders were princes,
   whose merchants,
        men honoured in the city?
9 Yahweh Sabaoth took this decision
   to wither the pride of all beauty
   and humiliate those honoured in the city.
10 Cultivate your country like the Delta,
        daughter of Tarshish,
   for your marine docks are no more.

¹¹ He has raised his hand against the sea,
    he has shaken kingdoms,
    Yahweh has ordained the destruction
    of the fortresses of Canaan.

¹² He has said, 'Exult no more,
    ill-treated virgin daughter of Sidon!
    Get up, cross to Kittim,
    no respite for you there, either.'
¹³ Look at the land of the Chaldaeans,
    a people who used not to exist!
    Assyria assigned it
        to the creatures of the wilds;
    they raised their siege-towers against it,
    demolished its bastions,
    reduced it to ruin.
¹⁴ Howl, ships of Tarshish,
        for your fortress has been destroyed.

¹⁵When that day comes, Tyre will be forgotten for seventy years, the length of one king's life. But when the seventy years are over, Tyre will become like the whore in the song:

¹⁶ 'Take your harp, walk the town,
    whore whom men have forgotten!
    Play sweetly, song after song,
    to make them remember you.'

¹⁷At the end of the seventy years Yahweh will visit Tyre. She will receive her pay again and play the whore with all the kingdoms of the world on the surface of the earth. ¹⁸But her profits and wages will be dedicated to Yahweh. They will not be stored or hoarded, but her profits will go to those who live in Yahweh's presence, for them to have as much food as they want and splendid clothes.

Apocalypse

YAHWEH'S JUDGEMENT

24 See how Yahweh lays the earth waste,
makes it a desert, buckles its surface,
scatters its inhabitants,

2 priest and people alike, master and slave,
mistress and maid, seller and buyer,
lender and borrower, creditor and debtor.

3 Ravaged, ravaged the earth will be,
despoiled, despoiled,
for Yahweh has uttered this word.

4 The earth is mourning, pining away,
the pick of earth's people
are withering away.

5 The earth is defiled
by the feet of its inhabitants,

for they have transgressed the laws,
violated the decree,
    broken the everlasting covenant.
⁶ That is why the curse
    has consumed the earth
and its inhabitants pay the penalty,
that is why the inhabitants of the earth
    have been burnt up
and few people are left.

SONG ABOUT THE RUINED CITY

⁷ The new wine is mourning,
    the vine is withering away,
the once merry-hearted are sighing.
⁸ The cheerful sound of tambourines
    is silent,
the sound of revelling is over,
the cheerful sound of the harp is silent.
⁹ No more will they sing over their wine,
liquor will taste bitter to the drinker.
¹⁰ The city of nothingness is in ruins,
every house is shut, no one can enter.
¹¹ People shout in the streets
    to try to get wine;
all joy has vanished,
happiness has been banished
    from the country.

¹² Nothing but rubble in the city,
the gate has collapsed in ruins.
¹³ For at the heart of earth's life,
among the peoples,
it is as at the beating of the olive trees,
as at the gleaning of the grapes
when the grape harvest is over.
¹⁴ They raise their voices,
shouting for joy,
in Yahweh's honour
they shout from the west.
¹⁵ 'Yes, in the east, give glory to Yahweh,
in the islands of the sea,
to the name of Yahweh, God of Israel!'
¹⁶ We have heard psalms
from the remotest parts of earth,
'Glory to the Upright One!'

THE LAST BATTLE

But I thought, 'What an ordeal,
what an ordeal! What misery for me!'
The traitors have betrayed,
the traitors have acted
most treacherously.
¹⁷ Fear, the pit and the snare for you,
inhabitants of the city!
¹⁸ And whoever flees from the cry of fear

will fall into the pit,
and whoever climbs out of the pit
will be caught in the snare.
Yes, the sluice-gates above are open,
the foundations of the earth are quaking.
¹⁹ A cracking, the earth cracks open,
a jolting, the earth gives a jolt,
a lurching, the earth lurches
backwards and forwards.
²⁰ The earth will reel to and fro
like a drunkard,
it will be shaken like a shanty;
so heavy will be its sin on it,
it will fall, never to rise again.
²¹ When that day comes,
Yahweh will punish
the armies of the sky above
and on earth the kings of the earth;
²² they will be herded together,
herded together like prisoners
in a dungeon
and shut up in gaol,
and, after long years, punished.
²³ The moon will be confused
and the sun ashamed,
for Yahweh Sabaoth is king
on Mount Zion and in Jerusalem,
and the Glory will radiate on their elders.

A HYMN OF THANKSGIVING

25 Yahweh, you are my God,
I shall praise you to the heights,
    I shall praise your name;
for you have accomplished marvels,
plans long-conceived, faithfully, firmly.

2 For you have made the town
        a heap of stones,
the fortified city a ruin.
The foreigners' citadel is a city no longer,
it will never be rebuilt.

3 Hence mighty peoples will honour you,
the city of pitiless nations hold you in awe;

4 For you have been a refuge for the weak,
a refuge for the needy in distress,
a shelter from the storm,
shade from the heat;
for the breath of the pitiless
is like a winter storm.

5 Like heat in a dry land
you calm the foreigners' tumult;
as heat under the shadow of a cloud,
so the song of the pitiless dies away.

THE DIVINE BANQUET

6 On this mountain, for all peoples,
Yahweh Sabaoth is preparing
a banquet of rich food,
    a banquet of fine wines,
of succulent food, of well-strained wines.
7 On this mountain, he has destroyed
the veil which used to veil all peoples,
the pall enveloping all nations;
8 he has destroyed death for ever.
Lord Yahweh has wiped away the tears
    from every cheek;
he has taken his people's shame away
    everywhere on earth,
for Yahweh has spoken.

9 And on that day, it will be said,
'Look, this is our God,
in him we put our hope
    that he should save us,
this is Yahweh, we put our hope in him.
Let us exult and rejoice
    since he has saved us.'
10 For Yahweh's hand will rest
    on this mountain,
and Moab will be trodden under his feet
as straw is trodden into the dung-heap.

¹¹ He may stretch his hands wide
     on the mountain
like a swimmer stretching out his hands
     to swim.
But he will humble his pride
despite what his hands may attempt.
¹² And the impregnable fortress
     of your walls,
he has overthrown, laid low,
flung to the ground, in the dust.

A HYMN OF THANKSGIVING

26 That day, this song will be sung in Judah:

'We have a fortress city,
the walls and ramparts provide safety.
² Open the gates!
     Let the upright nation come in,
the nation that keeps faith!
³ This is the plan decreed:
     you will guarantee peace,
the peace entrusted to you.
⁴ Trust in Yahweh for ever,
for Yahweh is a rock for ever.
⁵ He has brought low
     the dwellers on the heights,
the lofty citadel;

he lays it low, brings it to the ground,
flings it down in the dust.
⁶ It will be trodden under foot,
by the feet of the needy,
the steps of the weak.'

A PSALM

⁷ The path of the Upright One is honesty;
you smooth the honest way of the upright.
⁸ Following the path of your judgements,
Yahweh, we set our hopes in you,
your name, your memory
are all our soul desires.
⁹ At night my soul longs for you
and my spirit within me seeks you out;
for when your judgements appear on earth
the inhabitants of the world
learn what saving justice is.
¹⁰ If pity is shown to the wicked
without his learning what saving justice is,
he will act wrongly
in the land of right conduct
and not see the majesty of Yahweh.
¹¹ Yahweh, your hand is raised
but they do not see!
The antagonists of your people
will look and grow pale;

with your fiery wrath
    you will devour your enemies.

12 Yahweh, you will grant us peace,
    having completed all our undertakings
        for us.
13 Yahweh our God, other lords than you
        have ruled us
    but, loyal to you alone,
        we invoke your name.
14 The dead will not come back to life,
    the shadows will not rise again,
    for you have punished them,
        annihilated them,
    wiping out their very memory.
15 You have made the nation larger, Yahweh,
    made the nation larger
        and won yourself glory,
    you have rolled back
        the frontiers of the country.

16 Yahweh, in distress they had recourse
        to you,
    they expended themselves in prayer,
    since your punishment was on them.
17 As a pregnant woman
        near her time of delivery
    writhes and cries out in her pangs,

so have we been, Yahweh, in your eyes:
¹⁸ we have been pregnant, we have writhed,
but we have given birth only to wind:
we have not given salvation to the earth,
no inhabitants for the world
    have been brought to birth.
¹⁹ Your dead will come back to life,
    your corpses will rise again.
Wake up and sing,
    you dwellers in the dust,
for your dew will be a radiant dew,
but the earth will give birth to the shades.

THE LORD'S JUDGEMENT

²⁰ Go, my people, go to your private room,
shut yourselves in.
Hide yourselves a little while
until the retribution has passed.

²¹ For see, Yahweh emerges
    from his dwelling
to punish the inhabitants of earth
    for their guilt;
and the earth will reveal the blood
    shed on it
and no longer hide its slain.

27

That day Yahweh will punish,
with his unyielding sword,
massive and strong,
Leviathan the fleeing serpent,
Leviathan the coiling serpent;
he will kill that dragon that lives in the sea.

YAHWEH'S VINEYARD

2 That day,
sing of the splendid vineyard!

3 I, Yahweh, am its guardian,
from time to time I water it;
so that no harm befall it,
I guard it night and day.

4 —I do not have a wall.
Who can reduce me to brambles
and thorn-bushes?
—I shall make war and trample on it
and at the same time burn it.

5 Or should they beg for my protection,
let them make their peace with me,

PARDON AND PUNISHMENT

⁶ In days to come, Jacob will take root,
    Israel will bud and blossom
    and the surface of the world
        be one vast harvest.
⁷ Has he struck him as he was struck
        by those who struck him?
    Has he murdered him
        as he was murdered
            by those who murdered him?
⁸ By expelling, by excluding him,
        you have executed a sentence,
    he has blown him away with a breath
        as rough as the east wind.
⁹ For that is how Jacob's guilt
        will be forgiven,
    such will be the result
        of renouncing his sin,
    when all the altar-stones
        have been smashed to pieces
    like lumps of chalk,
    when the sacred poles and incense-altars
        stand no longer.
¹⁰ For the fortified city is abandoned now,
    deserted, forsaken as a desert
    where calves browse,
        where they lie down,

destroying its branches.
¹¹ When boughs go dry, they get burnt,
women come and use them for firewood.
Now, this is a people
that does not understand,
and so its Maker will not take pity on it,
he who formed it
will not show it any mercy.

THE ISRAELITES RETURN

¹² When that day comes,
Yahweh will start his threshing
from the course of the River
to the Torrent of Egypt,
and you will be gathered one by one,
Israelites!
¹³ When that day comes,
the great ram's-horn will be sounded,
and those lost in Assyria will come,
and those banished to Egypt,
and they will worship Yahweh
on the holy mountain, in Jerusalem.

Poems on Israel and Judah

AGAINST SAMARIA

28 Woe to the haughty crown
of Ephraim's drunkards,
to the fading flower
of its proud splendour
sited at the head of the lush valley,
to those prostrated by wine!

2 See, a strong and mighty man
in the Lord's service,
like a storm of hail, a destroying tempest,
like immense flood-waters overflowing,
with his hand he throws them
to the ground.

3 They will be trampled underfoot,
the haughty crown
of Ephraim's drunkards,

4 and the faded flower of its proud splendour
sited at the head of the lush valley.
Like a fig ripe before summer comes:
whoever spots it
forthwith picks and swallows it.

5 That day Yahweh Sabaoth
will be a crown of splendour

and a proud diadem
for the remnant of his people,
6 a spirit of fair judgement,
for him who sits in judgement,
and the strength of those
who repel the assault on the gate.

AGAINST FALSE PROPHETS

7 These too have been confused by wine,
have gone astray owing to liquor.
Priest and prophet have become
    confused by liquor,
are sodden with wine,
    have strayed owing to liquor,
have become confused in their visions,
have strayed in their decisions.
8 Yes, every table is covered
    in filthy vomit,
not one is clean!
9 'Whom does he think he is lecturing?
Whom does he think his message is for?
Babies just weaned?
Babies just taken from the breast?
10 With his
"Sav lasav, sav lasav,
kav lakav, kav lakav,
zeer sham, zeer sham!"'

¹¹ Now, with stammering lips
and in a foreign language,
he will talk to this nation.
¹² He used to say to them,
'Here you can rest!
Here you can let the weary rest!
Here all is quiet.'
But they refused to listen.
¹³ Now Yahweh is going to say this to them,
'Sav lasav, sav lasav,
kav lakav, kav lakav,
zeer sham, zeer sham.'
So that when they walk
they will fall over backwards
and so be broken, trapped
and taken captive.

AGAINST EVIL COUNSELLORS

¹⁴ Hence listen to Yahweh's word,
you insolent men,
rulers of this people in Jerusalem.
¹⁵ Because you have said,
'We have made a treaty with Death
and have struck a pact with Sheol.
When the scourging flood comes over,
it will not touch us,
for we have made lies our refuge

and hidden under falsehood.'
¹⁶ So the Lord Yahweh says this,
'Now I shall lay a stone in Zion,
a granite stone, a precious corner-stone,
a firm foundation-stone:
no one who relies on this will stumble.
¹⁷ And I will make fair judgement
    the measure,
and uprightness the plumb-line.'

But hail will sweep away the refuge of lies
and floods wash away the hiding-place;
¹⁸ your treaty with Death will be broken
and your pact with Sheol will not hold.
When the scourging flood comes over,
you will be trodden down by it;
¹⁹ every time it comes over,
    it will seize on you,
for it will come over,
    morning after morning,
day by day and night by night.
Nothing but fear
    will make you understand
        what you hear.
²⁰ For the bed is too short to stretch in,
the blanket too narrow for covering.
²¹ Yes, as on Mount Perazim,
    Yahweh will rise,

as in the Valley of Gibeon, he will storm
to do his work, his mysterious work,
to do his deed, his extraordinary deed.
²² Stop scoffing, then,
or your bonds will be tightened further,
for I have heard it:
it has been irrevocably decided
as regards the whole country
by the Lord Yahweh Sabaoth.

A PARABLE

²³ Listen closely to my words,
be attentive,
understand what I am saying.
²⁴ Does the ploughman
plough all day to sow,
breaking up and harrowing his ground?
²⁵ Once he has levelled its surface,
does he not scatter fennel, sow cummin?
Then he puts in wheat, millet, barley
and, round the edges, spelt,
²⁶ for his God has taught him this rule
and instructed him.
²⁷ Fennel must not be crushed
with a sledge,
nor cart-wheels driven over cummin;
fennel must be beaten with a stick,

and cummin with a flail.
²⁸ When you are threshing wheat,
you do not waste time crushing it;
you get the horse
and cart-wheel moving,
but you do not grind it fine.
²⁹ All this is a gift from Yahweh Sabaoth,
marvellous advice
leading to great achievements.

ON JERUSALEM

29 Woe, Ariel, Ariel,
city where David encamped.
Let year after year pass,
let the feasts make their full round,
² then I shall inflict trouble on Ariel,
and there will be sighing and sobbing,
and I shall make it truly Ariel.
³ I shall encamp all round you,
I shall lay siege to you
and mount siege-works against you.
⁴ You will be laid low,
will speak from the underworld,
your words will rise like a murmur
from the dust.
Your voice from the earth
will be like a ghost's,

it will whisper
as though coming from the dust.

5   The horde of your enemies
will be like fine dust,
the horde of the warriors like flying chaff.
And suddenly, in an instant,
6   you will be visited by Yahweh Sabaoth
with thunder, earthquake, mighty din,
hurricane, tempest,
flame of devouring fire.
7   It will be like a dream,
like a vision at night:
the horde of all the nations
at war with Ariel,
all those fighting,
besieging and troubling it.
8   It will be like the dream of a hungry man:
he eats, then wakes up with an empty belly;
or like the dream of a thirsty man:
he drinks, then wakes up exhausted
with a parched throat.
So will it be with the horde of all the nations
making war on Mount Zion.

9   Be stupefied and stunned,
go blind, unseeing,
drunk but not on wine,
staggering but not through liquor.

¹⁰ For Yahweh has infused you
   with a spirit of lethargy,
he has closed your eyes (the prophets),
he has veiled your heads (the seers).

¹¹For to you every vision has become like the words of
a sealed book. You give it to someone able to read and say,
'Read that.' He replies, 'I cannot, because it is sealed.' ¹²You
then give the book to someone who cannot read, and say,
'Read that.' He replies, 'I cannot read.'

PROPHECY

¹³ The Lord then said:
   Because this people approaches me
      only in words,
   honours me only with lip-service
   while their hearts are far from me,
   and reverence for me,
      as far as they are concerned,
   is nothing but human commandment,
      a lesson memorised,
¹⁴ very well, I shall have to go on
   astounding this people
      with prodigies and wonders:
   for the wisdom of its wise men is doomed,
   the understanding of any who understand
   will vanish.

THE TRIUMPH OF RIGHT

¹⁵ Woe to those who burrow down
to conceal their plans from Yahweh,
who scheme in the dark
and say, 'Who can see us?
Who knows who we are?'
¹⁶ How perverse you are!
Is the potter no better than the clay?
Something that was made,
can it say of its maker,
'He did not make me'?
Or a pot say of the potter,
'He does not know his job'?
¹⁷ Is it not true that in a very short time
the Lebanon
will become productive ground,
so productive you might take it
for a forest?
¹⁸ That day the deaf
will hear the words of the book
and, delivered from shadow and darkness,
the eyes of the blind will see.
¹⁹ The lowly will find ever more joy
in Yahweh
and the poorest of people
will delight in the Holy One of Israel;
²⁰ for the tyrant will be no more,

the scoffer has vanished
and all those on the look-out for evil
    have been destroyed:
²¹ those who incriminate others
        by their words,
those who lay traps for the arbitrator
        at the gate
and groundlessly deprive the upright
        of fair judgement.
²² That is why Yahweh,
        God of the House of Jacob,
Abraham's redeemer, says this,
'No longer shall Jacob be disappointed,
no more shall his face grow pale,
²³ for when he sees his children,
my creatures, home again with him,
he will acknowledge my name as holy,
he will acknowledge
        the Holy One of Jacob to be holy
and will hold the God of Israel in awe.
²⁴ Erring spirits will learn to understand and murmurers
    accept instruction.'

AGAINST THE EMBASSY TO EGYPT

30 Woe to the rebellious children—
        declares Yahweh—
    who make plans

which do not come from me
and make alliances not inspired by me,
and so add sin to sin!
2 They are leaving for Egypt,
without consulting me,
to take refuge in Pharaoh's protection,
to shelter in Egypt's shadow.
3 Pharaoh's protection will be your shame,
the shelter of Egypt's shadow
your confounding.
4 For his princes have gone to Zoan
and his messengers have reached Hanes.
5 Everyone has been disappointed
by a people who cannot help,
who bring neither aid nor profit,
only disappointment and confusion.

ANOTHER PROPHECY AGAINST AN EMBASSY

6 Proclamation about the beasts of the Negeb:

Into the land of distress and of anguish,
of lioness and roaring lion,
of viper and flying dragon,
they bear their riches on donkeys' backs,
their treasures on camels' humps,
to a nation that cannot help:

7   Egypt, whose help is vain and futile;
    and so I call her 'Rahab-the-collapsed'.

TESTAMENT

8   Now go, inscribe this on a tablet,
    write it on a scroll,
    so that it may serve for time to come
    for ever and for ever.
9   This is a rebellious people,
        they are lying children,
    children who will not listen
        to Yahweh's Law.
10 To the seers they say, 'See nothing!'
    To the prophets, 'Do not prophesy
        the truth to us;
    tell us flattering things;
        have illusory visions;
11 turn aside from the way, leave the path,
    rid us of the Holy One of Israel.'

12 So the Holy One of Israel says this,
    'Since you have rejected this word
        and put your trust in fraud
        and disloyalty
    and rely on these,
13 for you this guilt will prove to be
    a breach opening up,

a bulge at the top of a wall
which suddenly and all at once
comes crashing down.

¹⁴ He will shatter it like an earthenware pot,
ruthlessly knocking it to pieces,
so that of the fragments not one shard
can be found
with which to take up fire from the hearth
or scoop water from the storage-well.'

¹⁵ For Lord Yahweh, the Holy One of Israel,
says this,
'Your salvation lay in conversion
and tranquillity,
your strength in serenity and trust
and you would have none of it.

¹⁶ "No," you said, "we shall flee on horses."
And so flee you will!
And again, "We shall ride on swift ones."
And so your pursuers will be swift!

¹⁷ A thousand will quake at the threat of one
and when five threaten you will flee,
until what is left of you will be
like a flagstaff on a mountain top,
like a signal on a hill.'

GOD WILL FORGIVE

¹⁸ But Yahweh is waiting
to be gracious to you,

the Exalted One, to take pity on you,
for Yahweh is a God of fair judgement;
blessed are all who hope in him.

¹⁹ Yes, people of Zion living in Jerusalem,
you will weep no more.
He will be gracious to you
when your cry for help rings out;
as soon as he hears it,
he will answer you.
²⁰ When the Lord has given you
the bread of suffering
and the water of distress,
he who is your teacher will hide no longer,
and you will see your teacher
with your own eyes.
²¹ Your ears will hear these words
behind you,
'This is the way, keep to it,'
whether you turn to right or left.
²² You will hold unclean
the silverplating of your idols
and the goldplating of your images.
You will throw them away
like the polluted things they are,
shouting after them, 'Good riddance!'
²³ He will send rain
for the seed you sow in the ground,

and the bread that the ground provides
    will be rich and nourishing.
That day, your cattle will graze
    in wide pastures.
24 Oxen and donkeys that work the land
    will eat for fodder wild sorrel,
spread by the shovel-load and fork-load.
25 On every lofty mountain,
    on every high hill
there will be streams and water-courses,
    on the day of the great slaughter
when the strongholds fall.
26 Then moonlight will be
    bright as sunlight
and sunlight itself be
    seven times brighter
—like the light of seven days in one—
on the day Yahweh dresses
    his people's wound
and heals the scars of the blows
    they have received.

AGAINST ASSYRIA

27 See, the name of Yahweh
    comes from afar,
blazing his anger, heavy his threat.
His lips are brimming over with fury,

his tongue is like a devouring fire.

²⁸ His breath is like a river in spate
coming up to the neck,
to sift the nations
with the sieve of destruction,
to harness the peoples in a bridle,
that will lead them astray.

²⁹ Your song will be like that
on a festal night,
and there will be joy in your hearts
as when to the sound of the flute
people make a pilgrimage
to the mountain of Yahweh,
the Rock of Israel.

³⁰ Yahweh will make his majestic voice
ring out,
he will show the weight of his arm
in the heat of his anger,
with a devouring fire,
with thunderbolt,
downpour and hailstones.

³¹ Yes, at Yahweh's voice
Assyria will be terrified,
he will strike him with his rod;

³² each time he goes by,
will fall the punishing rod
that Yahweh will lay on him,
to the sound of tambourines and harps,

in the battles which he will wage
   against him with uplifted hand.
³³ Yes, Topheth has been ready
for a long time now,
that too is ready for the king,
deep and wide his pyre,
fire and wood in plenty.
Yahweh's breath,
   like a stream of brimstone,
will set fire to it.

AGAINST THE EGYPTIAN ALLIANCE

31 Woe to those going down to Egypt
for help,
who put their trust in horses,
who rely on the quantity of chariots,
and on great strength of cavalrymen,
but do not look to the Holy One of Israel
or consult Yahweh.
² Yet he too is wise and can bring disaster
and he will not go back on his word;
he will rise against the breed of evil-doers
and against those
   who protect wrong-doers.
³ The Egyptian is human, not divine,
his horses are flesh, not spirit;
Yahweh will stretch out his hand:

the protector will stumble,
the protected will fall
and all will perish together.

AGAINST ASSYRIA

⁴ Yes, this is what Yahweh has said to me:
As a lion or lion cub
growls over its prey,
when scores of shepherds
are summoned to drive it off,
without being frightened
by their shouting
or cowed by the noise they make,
just so will Yahweh Sabaoth descend
to fight for Mount Zion and for its hill.
⁵ Like hovering birds,
so will Yahweh Sabaoth
protect Jerusalem;
by protecting it, he will save it,
by supporting it, he will deliver it.
⁶ Come back to the one whom the Israelites
have so deeply betrayed!
⁷ For, that day, each of you will throw away
the false gods of silver
and the false gods of gold
which your own sinful hands have made.
⁸ Assyria will fall by the sword,

not that of a man,
will be devoured by the sword,
    of no human being,
he will flee before the sword
and his young warriors will be enslaved.
9 In his terror he will abandon his rock,
and his panic-stricken officers
    desert the standard—
declares Yahweh, whose fire is in Zion,
whose furnace, in Jerusalem.

A GOOD KING

32 There will be a king
who reigns uprightly
and princes who rule with fair judgement;
2 each will be like a shelter from the wind,
a refuge from the storm,
like streams on arid ground,
like the shade of a solid rock
    in a desolate land.
3 The eyes of seers will no longer be closed,
the ears of hearers will be alert,
4 the heart of the hasty
    will learn to think things over,
and the tongue of stammerers
    will speak promptly and clearly.

⁵ The fool will no longer be called generous,
  nor the rascal be styled bountiful.

NIGGARD AND NOBLE

⁶ For the fool speaks folly
  and his heart is set on villainy;
  he is godless in his actions
  and his words ascribe error to Yahweh;
  he starves the hungry of their food
  and refuses drink to the thirsty.
⁷ Everything to do with the rascal is evil,
  he devises infamous plans
  to ruin the poor with lying words
  even when the needy
    has right on his side;
⁸ but the noble person
    plans only noble things,
  noble his every move.

AGAINST THE WOMEN OF JERUSALEM

⁹ Stand up, you haughty women,
    listen to my words;
  you over-confident daughters,
    pay attention to what I say.

¹⁰ Within one year and a few days
   you will tremble,
      you over-confident women;
   grape-harvesting will be finished,
   gathering will never happen again.

¹¹ Shudder, you haughty women,
   tremble, you over-confident women;
   strip, undress, put sackcloth
      round your waists.

¹² Beat your breasts for the pleasant fields,
   for the fruitful vine,
¹³ for my people's soil
      where the bramble-bush will be growing
   and for all the happy houses,
      for the rejoicing city.

¹⁴ For the citadel will be abandoned
   and the thronged city deserted,
   Ophel and the Keep
      will be denuded for ever,
   the playground of wild donkeys
      and the pasture of flocks,

OUTPOURING OF THE SPIRIT

¹⁵ until the spirit is poured out on us
 from above,
and the desert becomes an orchard,
and an orchard that seems like a forest.

¹⁶ Fair judgement will fix its home
 in the desert,
And uprightness live in the productive ground,
¹⁷ And the product of uprightness will be peace,
The effect of uprightness
 being quiet and security for ever.

¹⁸ My people will live in a peaceful home,
In peaceful houses, tranquil dwellings.
And should the forest
 be totally destroyed
and the city gravely humiliated,
¹⁹ You will be happy to sow
 wherever there is water
And to let the ox and donkey roam free.

THE EXPECTED DELIVERANCE

33 Woe to you, destroying
though not yourself destroyed,

betraying though not yourself betrayed;
when you have finished destroying
　　you will be destroyed,
when you have stopped betraying
　　you will be betrayed.

2　Yahweh, show us your mercy,
we hope in you.
Be our arm every morning
and our salvation in time of stress.

3　At the sound of tumult the peoples flee,
When you stand up the nations scatter.

4　Your spoil is gathered in
　　as a grasshopper gathers in,
like a swarm of locusts
　　people descend on it.

5　Yahweh is exalted,
　　for he is enthroned above,
he has filled Zion with fair judgement
　　and saving justice.

6　You can count on this all your days:
wisdom and knowledge
　　are the riches that save,
the fear of Yahweh is his treasure.

7　Look, Ariel is lamenting in the streets,
the ambassadors of peace
　　are weeping bitterly.

8 The highways are deserted,
  no travellers any more on the roads.
  Agreements are broken,
      witnesses held in contempt,
  there is respect for no one.

9 The land pines away in mourning,
  the Lebanon is withering with shame,
  Sharon has become like the wasteland,
  Bashan and Carmel are shuddering.

10 'Now I shall stand up,' says Yahweh,
  'now I shall rise, now draw myself up.

11 You conceive chaff, you give birth to straw:
  like fire, my breath will devour you.

12 The peoples will be burnt up
      as though by quicklime,
  like cut thorns they will be burnt
      on the fire.

13 You who are far away,
      listen to what I have done,
  and you who are near, realise my strength.'

14 The sinners in Zion are panic-stricken
  and fear seizes on the godless,
  'Which of us can survive
      the devouring fire,
  Which of us survive everlasting burning?'

15 The one who acts uprightly
      and speaks honestly,
  who scorns to get rich by extortion,

who rejects bribes out of hand,
who refuses to listen to plans
    involving bloodshed
and shuts his eyes rather than countenance crime:
¹⁶ such a man will live on the heights,
the craggy rocks will be his refuge,
he will be fed, he will not want for water.

THE RETURN TO JERUSALEM

¹⁷ Your eyes will gaze on the king
    in his beauty,
they will look on a country
    stretching far and wide.
Your heart will meditate on past terrors,
'Where is the man who did the counting?
Where is the man who did the weighing?
Where is the man
    who counted off the towers?'
¹⁹ No more will you see that insolent people,
that people of unintelligible speech,
of barbarous and meaningless tongue.
²⁰ Gaze at Zion, city of our feasts;
Your eyes will see Jerusalem
as a home that is secure,
a tent not to be moved,
none of its tent-pegs ever to be pulled out,
none of its guy-ropes ever to be broken.

²¹ There it is that Yahweh
    shows us his power,
    like a place of rivers and very wide canals
    On which will row no galley,
    Over which will pass no majestic ship.

²² (For Yahweh is our judge,
    Yahweh our lawgiver,
    Yahweh is our king and our Saviour.)
²³ Your tackle has given way,
    it cannot support the mast,
    it cannot hoist the pennon.
    And so there is much booty
        to be shared out;
    the lame fall to plundering,
²⁴ and no one living there will say,
        'I am sickly';
    the people living there
        will find their guilt forgiven.

THE SENTENCE ON EDOM

34 Come near and listen, you nations,
    pay attention, you peoples.
    Let the earth and its contents listen,
    the world and its entire population.
² For Yahweh is angry with all the nations,
    enraged with all their hordes.

He has vowed them to destruction,
handed them over to slaughter.
3 Their dead will be thrown away,
the stench will rise from their corpses,
the mountains will run with their blood,
4 the entire array of heaven will fall apart.
The heavens will be rolled up like a scroll
and all their array will fade away,
as fade the leaves falling from the vine,
as fade those falling from the fig tree.

5 For my sword has drunk deep
in the heavens:
see how it now falls on Edom,
on the people vowed to destruction,
to punish them.
6 Yahweh's sword is gorged with blood,
it is greasy with fat,
with the blood of lambs and goats,
with the fat of the kidneys of rams.
For Yahweh has a sacrifice in Bozrah,
a great slaughter in the land of Edom.
7 The wild oxen will fall with them,
the bullocks with the bulls;
their land will be drenched with blood
and their dust will be greasy with fat.
8 For this will be Yahweh's day
of vengeance,

the year of retribution in Zion's lawsuit.

9 Its streams will turn into pitch,
   its dust into brimstone,
   its country will turn into blazing pitch.
10 Never quenched night or day,
   its smoke rising for ever,
   it will lie waste age after age,
   no one will travel through it
      for ever and ever.
11 It will be the haunt of pelican
      and hedgehog,
   the owl and the raven will live there;
   over it Yahweh will stretch
      the measuring line of chaos
   and the plumb-line of emptiness.

12 There will be no more nobles
   to proclaim the royal authority;
   there will be an end of all its princes.
13 Brambles will grow in its bastions,
   nettles and thorn-bushes in its fortresses,
   it will be the lair of jackals,
   an enclosure for ostriches.
14 Wild cats will meet hyenas there,
   satyr will call to satyr,
   there Lilith too will lurk
   and find somewhere to rest.

¹⁵ The snake will nest and lay eggs there,
   will hatch and gather its young
      into the shade;
   and there the vultures will assemble,
   each one with its mate.
¹⁶ Search in Yahweh's book, and read,
   not one of these will be missing,
   not one of them lacking a mate;
   for thus his mouth has ordained it,
   and his spirit has brought them together.
¹⁷ He has thrown the lot for each,
   his hand has measured out their share;
   they will possess it for ever,
   and live there age after age.

THE TRIUMPH OF JERUSALEM

35 Let the desert and the dry lands
   be glad,
   let the wasteland rejoice and bloom;
   like the asphodel, ²let it burst into flower,
   let it rejoice and sing for joy.
   The glory of Lebanon is bestowed on it,
   the splendour of Carmel and Sharon;
   then they will see the glory of Yahweh,
   the splendour of our God.
³ Strengthen all weary hands,

steady all trembling knees
4 and say to the faint-hearted,
'Be strong! Do not be afraid.
Here is your God,
vengeance is coming,
divine retribution;
he is coming to save you.'
5 Then the eyes of the blind
will be opened,
the ears of the deaf unsealed,
6 then the lame will leap like a deer
and the tongue of the dumb sing for joy;
for water will gush in the desert
and streams in the wastelands,
7 the parched ground will become a marsh
and the thirsty land springs of water;
the lairs where the jackals used to live
will become plots of reed and papyrus.

8 And through it will run a road for them
and a highway
which will be called the Sacred Way;
the unclean will not be allowed to use it;
He will be the one to use this road,
the fool will not stray along it.
9 No lion will be there,
no ferocious beast set foot on it,
nothing of the sort be found;

it will be used by the redeemed.
¹⁰ For those whom Yahweh has ransomed
will return,
they will come to Zion shouting for joy,
their heads crowned with joy unending;
rejoicing and gladness will escort them
and sorrow and sighing will take flight.

Appendices

SENNACHERIB'S INVASION

36 In the fourteenth year of King Hezekiah, Sennacherib king of Assyria advanced on all the fortified towns of Judah and captured them.²From Lachish the king of Assyria sent the cupbearer-in-chief with a large force to King Hezekiah in Jerusalem. The cupbearer-in-chief took up position near the conduit of the upper pool on the road to the Fuller's Field.³The master of the palace, Eliakim son of Hilkiah, Shebna the secretary and the herald Joah son of Asaph went out to him. ⁴The cupbearer-in-chief said to them, 'Say to Hezekiah, "The great king, the king of Assyria, says this: What makes you so confident? ⁵Do you think empty words are as good as strategy and military strength? Who are you relying on, to dare to rebel against me? ⁶There you are, relying on that broken reed, Egypt, which pricks and pierces the hand of the person who leans on it. That is what Pharaoh king of Egypt is like to all who rely on him. ⁷You may say to me: We rely on Yahweh our God. But haven't his high places and altars been suppressed by Hezekiah, who told Judah and Jerusalem: This is the altar before which you must worship? ⁸Very well, then, make a wager with my lord the king of Assyria: I will give you two thousand horses if you can find horsemen to ride them. ⁹How could you repulse a single one of the least of my master's soldiers? And yet you have relied on Egypt for chariots and horsemen. ¹⁰And lastly, have I marched on this country to lay it waste without warrant from Yahweh? Yahweh himself said to me: March on this country and lay it waste." '

¹¹Eliakim, Shebna and Joah said to the cupbearer-in-chief, 'Please speak to your servants in Aramaic, for we understand it; do not speak to us in the Judaean language within earshot of the people on the ramparts.' ¹²But the cupbearer-in-chief said, 'Do you think my lord sent me here to say these things to your master or to you? On the contrary, it was to the people sitting on the ramparts who, like you, are doomed to eat their own dung and drink their own urine.'

¹³The cupbearer-in-chief then drew himself up and shouted loudly in the Judaean language, 'Listen to the words of the great king, the king of Assyria. ¹⁴The king says this, "Do not let Hezekiah delude you! He will be powerless to save you. ¹⁵Do not let Hezekiah persuade you

to rely on Yahweh by saying: Yahweh is sure to save us; this city will not fall into the king of Assyria's clutches. [16]Do not listen to Hezekiah, for the king of Assyria says this: Make peace with me, [17]surrender to me, and every one of you will be free to eat the fruit of his own vine and of his own fig tree and to drink the water of his own storage-well until I come and take you away to a country like your own, a land of corn and good wine, a land of bread and vineyards. [18]Do not let Hezekiah delude you by saying: Yahweh will save us. Has any god of any nation been able to save his country from the king of Assyria's clutches? [19]Where are the gods of Hamath and Arpad? Where are the gods of Sepharvaim? Where are the national gods of Samaria? Did they save Samaria from my clutches? [20]Of all the national gods, which ones have saved their countries from my clutches, that Yahweh should be able to save Jerusalem from my clutches?" '

[21]They, however, kept quiet and said nothing in reply, since the king had given the order, 'You are not to answer him.' [22]The master of the palace, Eliakim son of Hilkiah, Shebna the secretary and the herald Joah son of Asaph, with their clothes torn, went to Hezekiah and reported what the cupbearer-in-chief had said.

THE PROPHET ISAIAH IS CONSULTED

37 On hearing this, King Hezekiah tore his clothes, put on sackcloth and went to the

Temple of Yahweh. ²He sent Eliakim master of the palace, Shebna the secretary and the elders of the priests, wearing sackcloth, to the prophet Isaiah son of Amoz. ³They said to him, 'This is what Hezekiah says, "Today is a day of suffering, of punishment, of disgrace. Children come to birth and there is no strength to bring them forth. ⁴May Yahweh your God hear the words of the cupbearer-in-chief whom his master, the king of Assyria, has sent to insult the living God, and may Yahweh your God punish the words he has heard! Offer your prayer for the remnant still left." '

⁵When King Hezekiah's ministers came to Isaiah, ⁶he said to them, 'Say to your master, "Yahweh says this: Do not be afraid of the words which you have heard or the blasphemies which the king of Assyria's minions have uttered against me. ⁷Look, I am going to put a spirit in him and, on the strength of a rumour, he will go back to his own country, and in that country I shall make him fall by the sword." '

THE CUPBEARER RETURNS TO HIS MASTER

⁸The cupbearer turned about and rejoined the king of Assyria, who was then attacking Libnah, the cupbearer having learnt that the king had already left Lachish ⁹on hearing that Tirhakah king of Cush was on his way to attack him.

SECOND ACCOUNT OF
SENNACHERIB'S ACTIVITIES

Sennacherib again sent messengers to Hezekiah, saying, [10]'Tell Hezekiah king of Judah this, "Do not let your God on whom you are relying deceive you with the promise: Jerusalem will not fall into the king of Assyria's clutches. [11]You have learnt by now what the kings of Assyria have done to all the other countries, putting them under the curse of destruction. Are you likely to be saved? [12]Did the gods of the nations whom my ancestors devastated save them—Gozan, Haran, Rezeph and the Edenites who were in Tel Basar? [13]Where is the king of Hamath, the king of Arpad, the king of Lair, of Sepharvaim, of Hena, of Ivvah?" '

[14]Hezekiah took the letter from the messengers' hands and read it; he then went up to the Temple of Yahweh and spread it out before Yahweh. [15]Hezekiah said this prayer in the presence of Yahweh, [16]'Yahweh Sabaoth, God of Israel, enthroned on the winged creatures, you alone are God of all the kingdoms of the world, you made heaven and earth. [17]Give ear, Yahweh, and listen; open your eyes, Yahweh, and see! Hear the words of Sennacherib, who has sent to insult the living God. [18]It is true, Yahweh, that the kings of Assyria have destroyed all the nations (and their countries); [19]they have thrown their gods on the fire, for these were not gods but human artefacts—wood and stone—and hence they have destroyed them. [20]But now,

Yahweh our God, save us from his clutches, I beg you, and let all the kingdoms of the world know that you alone are God, Yahweh.'

ISAIAH INTERVENES

[21]Isaiah son of Amoz then sent the following message to Hezekiah, 'Yahweh, God of Israel, says this, "In answer to the prayer which you have addressed to me about Sennacherib king of Assyria. [22]Here is the pronouncement which Yahweh has made about him:

> She despises you, she scorns you,
>   the virgin daughter of Zion;
> she tosses her head at you,
>   the daughter of Jerusalem!
> [23] Whom have you insulted,
>   whom did you blaspheme?
>   Against whom raised your voice
>   and lifted your haughty eyes?
>   Against the Holy One of Israel.
> [24] Through your minions
>   you have insulted the Lord,
>   thinking: With my many chariots
>   I have climbed the mountain-tops,
>   the utmost peaks of Lebanon.
>   I have felled its mighty cedars,
>   its finest cypresses,

have reached its furthest peak,
its forest garden.
²⁵ Yes, I have dug and drunk
of foreign waters;
under the soles of my feet
I have dried up all Egypt's rivers.

²⁶ Do you hear? Long ago
I prepared this,
from days of old
I actually planned it,
now I carry it out.
You were to lay walled cities
in heaps of ruins;
²⁷ that was why their inhabitants,
feeble of hand,
were dismayed and discomfited,
were weak as grass,
were frail as plants,
were like grass of housetop and meadow
under the east wind.
²⁸ But whether you stand up or sit down,
whether you go out or come in, I know it
(and how you rave against me).
²⁹ Because you have raved against me
and your arrogance has reached my ears,
I shall put a hook through your nostrils
and a muzzle on your lips,

and make you return by the road
by which you came.

A SIGN FOR HEZEKIAH

30 And this will be the sign for you:
This year will be eaten the self-sown grain,
next year what sprouts in the fallow;
but in the third year sow and reap,
plant vineyards and eat their fruit.
31 The surviving remnant
of the House of Judah will bring forth
new roots below and fruits above;
32 for a remnant will issue from Jerusalem,
and survivors from Mount Zion.
Yahweh Sabaoth's jealous love
will accomplish this." '

A PROPHECY ON ASSYRIA

33"This, then, is what Yahweh says about the king of Assyria:

He will not enter this city,
will shoot no arrow at it,
confront it with no shield,
throw up no earthwork against it.
34 By the road by which he came,
by that he will return;

he will not enter this city,
> declares Yahweh.

35 I shall protect this city and save it
> for my sake and my servant David's sake.'

SENNACHERIB IS PUNISHED

36That same night the angel of Yahweh went out and struck down a hundred and eighty-five thousand men in the Assyrian camp. In the early morning when it was time to get up, there they lay, so many corpses.

37Sennacherib struck camp and left; he returned home and stayed in Nineveh.38One day when he was worshipping in the temple of his god Nisroch, his sons Adrammelech and Sharezer struck him down with the sword and escaped into the territory of Ararat. His son Esarhaddon succeeded him.

THE ILLNESS AND CURE OF HEZEKIAH

38 About then, Hezekiah fell ill and was at the point of death. The prophet Isaiah son of Amoz came and said to him, 'Yahweh says this, "Put your affairs in order, for you are going to die, you will not live."' 2Hezekiah turned his face to the wall and addressed this prayer to Yahweh, 3'Ah, Yahweh, remember, I beg you, that I have behaved faithfully and with sincerity of heart in your presence and done what you regard as right.' And Hezekiah shed many tears.

[4]Then the word of Yahweh came to Isaiah, [5]'Go and say to Hezekiah, "Yahweh, the God of your ancestor David, says this: I have heard your prayer and seen your tears. I shall cure you: in three days' time you will go up to the Temple of Yahweh. I shall add fifteen years to your life. [6]I shall save you and this city from the king of Assyria's clutches and defend this city for my sake and my servant David's sake." '

[21]'Bring a fig poultice,' Isaiah said, 'apply it to the ulcer and he will recover.'[22]Hezekiah said, 'What is the sign to tell me that I shall be going up to the Temple of Yahweh?'[15] [7]'Here', Isaiah replied, 'is the sign from Yahweh that he will do what he has said. [8]Look, I shall make the shadow cast by the declining sun on the steps—the steps to Ahaz's roof-room—go back ten steps.' And the sun went back the ten steps by which it had declined.

THE CANTICLE OF HEZEKIAH

[9]Canticle of Hezekiah king of Judah after his illness and recovery.

[10] I thought: In the noon of my life
I am to depart.
At the gates of Sheol I shall be held
for the rest of my days.

¹¹ I thought: I shall never see Yahweh again
in the land of the living,
I shall never see again a single one
of those who live on earth.
¹² My home has been pulled up,
and thrown away
like a shepherd's tent;
like a weaver, I have rolled up my life,
he has cut me from the loom.
From dawn to dark,
you have been making an end of me;
¹³ till daybreak, I cried for help;
like a lion, he has crushed all my bones,
from dawn to dark,
you have been making an end of me.
¹⁴ I twitter like a swallow,
I moan like a dove,
my eyes have grown dim from looking up.
Lord, I am overwhelmed,
come to my help.
¹⁵ How can I speak
and what can I say to him?
He is the one to act.
I must eke out the rest of my years
in bitterness of soul.

¹⁶ The Lord is over them; they live,
and everything in them lives by his spirit.

You will cure me. Restore me to life.

¹⁷ At once, my bitterness turns to well-being.
For you have preserved my soul
from the pit of nothingness,
you have thrust all my sins behind you.

¹⁸ For Sheol cannot praise you,
nor Death celebrate you;
those who go down to the pit
can hope no longer in your constancy.

¹⁹ The living, the living are the ones
who praise you,
as I do today.
Fathers tell their sons
about your constancy.

²⁰ Yahweh, come to my help
and we will make our harps resound
all the days of our life
in the Temple of Yahweh.

THE BABYLONIAN EMBASSY

39 At that time, the king of Babylon, Merodach-Baladan son of Baladan, sent letters and a gift to Hezekiah, for he had heard of his illness and his recovery. ²Hezekiah was delighted at this and showed the ambassadors his entire treasury, the silver, gold, spices, precious oil, his armoury too, and everything to be seen in his storehouses. There was nothing in his

palace or in his whole domain that Hezekiah did not
show them.

³The prophet Isaiah then came to King Hezekiah and
asked him, 'What have these men said, and where have they
come to you from?' Hezekiah answered, 'They have come
from a distant country, from Babylon.' ⁴Isaiah said, 'What
have they seen in your palace?' 'They have seen everything
in my palace,' Hezekiah answered. 'There is nothing in my
storehouses that I have not shown them.'

⁵Then Isaiah said to Hezekiah, 'Listen to the word of
Yahweh Sabaoth, ⁶"The days are coming when everything
in your palace, everything that your ancestors have amassed
until now, will be carried off to Babylon. Not a thing will
be left," Yahweh says. ⁷"Sons sprung from you, sons
begotten by you, will be abducted to be eunuchs in the
palace of the king of Babylon." ' ⁸Hezekiah said to Isaiah,
'This word of Yahweh that you announce is reassuring,' for
he was thinking, 'There is going to be peace and security
during my lifetime.'

THE BOOK OF THE CONSOLATION OF ISRAEL

PREDICTION OF DELIVERANCE

40 'Console my people, console them,' says your God.

2 'Speak to the heart of Jerusalem
and cry to her
that her period of service is ended,
that her guilt has been atoned for,
that, from the hand of Yahweh,
    she has received
double punishment for all her sins.'

3 A voice cries, 'Prepare in the desert
a way for Yahweh.
Make a straight highway for our God
across the wastelands.
4 Let every valley be filled in,
every mountain and hill be levelled,
every cliff become a plateau,
every escarpment a plain;

⁵ then the glory of Yahweh will be revealed
and all humanity will see it together,
for the mouth of Yahweh has spoken.'

⁶ A voice said, 'Cry aloud!' and I said,
    'What shall I cry?'
—'All humanity is grass
and all its beauty like the wild flower's.
⁷ The grass withers, the flower fades
when the breath of Yahweh blows on them.
(The grass is surely the people.)
⁸ The grass withers, the flower fades,
but the word of our God remains for ever.'

⁹ Go up on a high mountain,
messenger of Zion.
Shout as loud as you can,
messenger of Jerusalem!
Shout fearlessly,
say to the towns of Judah,
'Here is your God.'

¹⁰ Here is Lord Yahweh coming with power,
his arm maintains his authority,
his reward is with him
and his prize precedes him.
¹¹ He is like a shepherd feeding his flock,
gathering lambs in his arms,

holding them against his breast
and leading to their rest the mother ewes.

THE MAJESTY OF GOD

¹² Who was it measured the water of the sea
    in the hollow of his hand
and calculated the heavens
    to the nearest inch,
gauged the dust of the earth
    to the nearest bushel,
weighed the mountains in scales,
the hills in a balance?

¹³ Who directed the spirit of Yahweh,
what counsellor could have
    instructed him?
¹⁴ Whom has he consulted to
    enlighten him,
to instruct him in the path of judgement,
to teach him knowledge
and show him how to understand?
¹⁵ See, the nations are like a drop
    in a bucket,
they count as a grain of dust
    on the scales.
See, coasts and islands
    weigh no more than fine powder.

¹⁶ The Lebanon is not enough
    for the burning fires
nor its animals enough
    for the burnt offering.
¹⁷ All the nations are as nothing
    before him,
for him they count as nothingness
    and emptiness.
¹⁸ To whom can you compare God?
What image can you contrive of him?

¹⁹ The craftsman casts an idol,
a goldsmith overlays it with gold
and casts silver chains for it.
²⁰ Someone too poor to afford a sacrifice
chooses a piece of wood
    that will not rot;
he then seeks out a skilled craftsman
to set up an idol that will not totter.
²¹ Did you not know,
had you not heard?
Was it not told you from the beginning?
Have you not understood
    how the earth was set on its foundations?
²² He who sits enthroned
    above the circle of the earth,
the inhabitants of which
    are like grasshoppers,

stretches out the heavens like a cloth,
spreads them out like a tent to live in.

23 He reduces princes to nothing,
the rulers of the world
to mere emptiness.

24 Scarcely are they planted,
scarcely sown,
scarcely has their stem
taken root in the soil,
than he blows on them and they wither
and the storm carries them away
like chaff.

25 'To whom can you compare me,
or who is my equal?'
says the Holy One.

26 Lift your eyes and look:
he who created these things
leads out their army in order,
summoning each of them by name.
So mighty is his power,
so great his strength,
that not one fails to answer.

27 How can you say, Jacob,
how can you repeat, Israel,
'My way is hidden from Yahweh,
my rights are ignored by my God'?

28 Did you not know? Had you not heard?

Yahweh is the everlasting God,
he created the remotest parts
of the earth.
He does not grow tired or weary,
his understanding is beyond fathoming.
²⁹ He gives strength to the weary,
he strengthens the powerless.
³⁰ Youths grow tired and weary,
the young stumble and fall,
³¹ but those who hope in Yahweh
will regain their strength,
they will sprout wings like eagles,
though they run
they will not grow weary,
though they walk they will never tire.

CYRUS, THE INSTRUMENT OF YAHWEH

41 Coasts and islands,
fall silent before me,
and let the peoples renew their strength,
let them come forward and speak;
let us assemble for judgement.
² 'Who has raised from the east
him whom saving justice
summons in its train,
him to whom Yahweh

delivers up the nations
and subjects kings,
him who reduces them to dust
    with his sword,
and to driven stubble with his bow,
3 him who pursues them
    and advances unhindered,
his feet scarcely touching the road?
4 Who has acted thus, who has done this?
He who calls each generation
    from the beginning:
I, Yahweh, who am the first
and till the last I shall still be there.'
5 The coasts and islands have seen
    and taken fright,
the remotest parts of earth are trembling:
they are approaching, they are here!
6 People help one another,
they say to each other, 'Take heart!'
7 The woodworker encourages the smelter,
the polisher encourages the hammerer,
saying of the soldering, 'It is sound';
and he fastens it with nails
to keep it steady.

ISRAEL, CHOSEN AND PROTECTED BY YAHWEH

⁸ But you, Israel, my servant,
Jacob whom I have chosen,
descendant of Abraham my friend,
⁹ whom I have taken to myself,
from the remotest parts of the earth
and summoned from countries far away,
to whom I have said, 'You are my servant,
I have chosen you, I have not rejected you,'
¹⁰ do not be afraid, for I am with you;
do not be alarmed, for I am your God.
I give you strength, truly I help you,
truly I hold you firm
with my saving right hand.
¹¹ Look, all those who rage against you
will be put to shame and humiliated;
those who picked quarrels with you
will be reduced to nothing and will perish.
¹² You will look for them
but will not find them,
those who used to fight you;
they will be destroyed
and brought to nothing,
those who made war on you.
¹³ For I, Yahweh, your God,
I grasp you by your right hand;

    I tell you, 'Do not be afraid,
    I shall help you.'

14 Do not be afraid, Jacob, you worm!
    You little handful of Israel!
    I shall help you, declares Yahweh;
    your redeemer is the Holy One of Israel.

15 Look, I am making you
    into a threshing-sledge,
    new, with double teeth;
    you will thresh
    and beat the mountains to dust
    and reduce the hills to straw.

16 You will winnow them
    and the wind will carry them off,
    the gale will scatter them;
    whereas you will rejoice in Yahweh,
    will glory in the Holy One of Israel.

17 The oppressed and needy
    search for water,
    and there is none,
    their tongue is parched with thirst.
    I, Yahweh, shall answer them,
    I, the God of Israel,
    shall not abandon them.

18 I shall open up rivers on barren heights
    and water-holes down in the ravines;
    I shall turn the desert into a lake
    and dry ground into springs of water.

¹⁹ I shall plant the desert with cedar trees,
  acacias, myrtles and olives;
  in the wastelands I shall put cypress trees,
  plane trees and box trees side by side;
²⁰ so that people may see and know,
  so that they may all observe
    and understand
  that the hand of Yahweh has done this,
  that the Holy One of Israel has created it.

THE FATUITY OF IDOLS

²¹ 'Present your case,' says Yahweh,
  'Produce your arguments,'
    says Jacob's king.
²² 'Let them produce and reveal to us
  what is going to happen.
  What happened in the past?
  Reveal it so that we can consider it
  and know what the outcome will be.
  Or tell us about the future,
²³ reveal what is to happen next,
  and then we shall know
    that you are gods.
  At least, do something,
    be it good or bad,
  so that we may feel alarm and fear.
²⁴ Look, you are less than nothingness,

and what you do is less than nothing;
to choose you is an outrage.'

25 I have raised him from the north
    and he has come,
from the east he has been summoned
    by name.
He tramples on rulers like mud,
like a potter treading clay.

26 Who revealed this from the beginning
    for us to know,
and in the past for us to say,
'That is right'?
No one in fact revealed it,
    no one proclaimed it,
no one has heard you speak.

27 First-fruits of Zion, look,
    here they come!
I send a messenger to Jerusalem,

28 and I look—no one,
not a single counsellor among them
who, if I asked, could give an answer.

29 Taken altogether they are nothingness,
what they do is nothing,
their statues, wind and emptiness.

FIRST SONG OF THE SERVANT

42 Here is my servant whom I uphold,
my chosen one
in whom my soul delights.
I have sent my spirit upon him,
he will bring fair judgement to the nations.

2 He does not cry out or raise his voice,
his voice is not heard in the street;

3 he does not break the crushed reed
or snuff the faltering wick.
Faithfully he presents fair judgement;

4 he will not grow faint,
he will not be crushed
until he has established
fair judgement on earth,
and the coasts and islands
are waiting for his instruction.

5 Thus says God, Yahweh,
who created the heavens
and spread them out,
who hammered into shape the earth
and what comes from it,
who gave breath to the people on it,
and spirit to those who walk on it:

6 I, Yahweh, have called you
in saving justice,

I have grasped you by the hand
 and shaped you;
I have made you a covenant of the people
and light to the nations,
7 to open the eyes of the blind,
to free captives from prison,
and those who live in darkness
 from the dungeon.
8 I am Yahweh, that is my name!
I shall not yield my glory to another,
nor my honour to idols.
9 See how the former predictions
 have come true.
Fresh things I now reveal;
before they appear I tell you of them.

SONG OF VICTORY

10 Sing a new song to Yahweh!
Let his praise be sung
 from remotest parts of the earth
by those who sail the sea
 and by everything in it,
by the coasts and islands
 and those who inhabit them.
11 Let the desert and its cities
 raise their voices,
the encampments where Kedar lives.

Let the inhabitants of the Rock
cry aloud for joy
and shout from the mountain tops.
¹² Let them give glory to Yahweh
and, in the coasts and islands,
let them voice his praise.
¹³ Yahweh advances like a hero,
like a warrior he rouses his fire.
He shouts, he raises the war cry,
he shows his might against his foes.
¹⁴ 'From long ago I have been silent,
I have kept quiet, held myself in check,
groaning like a woman in labour,
panting and gasping for air.
¹⁵ I shall ravage mountain and hill,
shall wither all their vegetation;
I shall turn the torrents into firm ground
and dry up the marshes.
¹⁶ I shall lead the blind by a road
they do not know,
by paths they do not know
I shall conduct them.
I shall turn the darkness into light
before them
and the quagmires into solid ground.
This I shall do—without fail.'
¹⁷ Those who trust in idols will recoil,
they will blush for shame,

who say to metal images,
'You are our gods.'

ISRAEL'S BLINDNESS

¹⁸ Listen, you deaf!
Look and see, you blind!
¹⁹ Who so blind as my servant,
so deaf as the messenger I send?
(Who so blind as the friend
I have taken to myself,
so deaf as Yahweh's servant?)
²⁰ You have seen many things
but not observed them;
your ears are open but you do not hear.
²¹ Yahweh wished,
because of his saving justice,
to make the Law great and glorious.
²² Yet here is a people pillaged
and plundered,
all of them shut up in caves,
imprisoned in dungeons.
They have been pillaged,
with no one to rescue them,
plundered, with, no one to say,
'Give it back!'
²³ Which of you will listen to this,
who pay attention and listen in future?

²⁴ Who surrendered Jacob
    to the plunderer
and Israel to the pillagers?
Was it not Yahweh, against whom
    we had sinned,
in whose ways they would not walk
and whose Law they would not obey?
²⁵ On him he poured out his blazing anger
and the fury of war;
it enveloped him in flames
    and yet he did not understand;
it burned him up,
    but he did not learn a lesson.

GOD, ISRAEL'S PROTECTOR AND LIBERATOR

43 And now,
    thus says Yahweh,
he who created you, Jacob,
who formed you, Israel:
Do not be afraid, for I have redeemed you;
I have called you by your name,
    you are mine.
² Should you pass through the waters,
    I shall be with you;
or through rivers,
    they will not swallow you up.

Should you walk through fire,
    you will not suffer,
and the flame will not burn you.

3 For I am Yahweh, your God,
    the Holy One of Israel, your Saviour.
I have given Egypt for your ransom,
Cush and Seba in exchange for you.

4 Since I regard you as precious,
    since you are honoured and I love you,
I therefore give people
    in exchange for you,
and nations in return for your life.

5 Do not be afraid, for I am with you.
I shall bring your offspring from the east,
    and gather you from the west.

6 To the north I shall say, 'Give them up!'
    and to the south, 'Do not hold them back!'
Bring back my sons from far away,
and my daughters from the remotest part
    of the earth,

7 everyone who bears my name,
    whom I have created for my glory,
whom I have formed, whom I have made.

YAHWEH ALONE IS GOD

8 Bring forward the people that is blind,
    yet has eyes,

that is deaf and yet has ears.

⁹ Let all the nations assemble,
let the peoples gather here!
Which of them has proclaimed this
and revealed things to us in the past?
Let them bring their witnesses
    to justify themselves,
let others hear and say, 'It is true.'

¹⁰ You yourselves are my witnesses,
    declares Yahweh,
and the servant whom I have chosen,
so that you may know and believe me
and understand that it is I.
    No god was formed before me,
nor will be after me.

¹¹ I, I am Yahweh,
and there is no other Saviour but me.

¹² I have revealed, have saved,
    and have proclaimed,
not some foreigner among you.
You are my witnesses,
    declares Yahweh,

I am God,¹³yes, from eternity I am.
No one can deliver from my hand;
when I act, who can thwart me?

AGAINST BABYLON

¹⁴ Thus says Yahweh,
   your redeemer, the Holy One of Israel:
   For your sake I have sent to Babylon,
   I shall knock down all the prison bars,
   and the Chaldaeans' shouts of joy
      will change to lamentations.
¹⁵ I am Yahweh, your Holy One,
   the Creator of Israel, your king.

MIRACLES OF THE NEW EXODUS

⁶ Thus says Yahweh,
   who made a way through the sea,
   a path in the raging waters,
¹⁷ who led out chariot and horse
   together with an army of picked troops:
   they lay down never to rise again,
   they were snuffed out, put out like a wick.
¹⁸ No need to remember past events,
   no need to think about
      what was done before.
¹⁹ Look, I am doing something new,
   now it emerges; can you not see it?
   Yes, I am making a road in the desert
   and rivers in wastelands.
²⁰ The wild animals will honour me,

the jackals and the ostriches,
for bestowing water in the desert
and rivers on the wastelands
for my people, my chosen one, to drink.
²¹ The people I have shaped for myself
will broadcast my praises.

ISRAEL'S INGRATITUDE

²² But, Jacob, you have not invoked me;
no, Israel, you have grown weary of me.
²³ You have not brought me lambs
    as your burnt offerings
and have not honoured me
    with your sacrifices.
I have not subjected you
    to cereal offering,
I have not wearied you
    by demanding incense.
²⁴ You have not bought expensive reed
    for me
or sated me with the fat
    of your sacrifices.
Instead by your sins
    you have treated me like a slave,
you have wearied me with your crimes,
²⁵ I, I it is who blot out your acts of revolt
    for my own sake

and shall not call your sins to mind.
26 Remind me,
  and we will judge this together;
state your own case and justify yourself.
27 Your first ancestor sinned,
your interpreters revolted against me.
28 That is why I deposed the chief men
  of my sanctuary,
why I put Jacob
  under the curse of destruction
and subjected Israel to insult.

THE BLESSING IN STORE FOR ISRAEL

44 And now listen, Jacob my servant,
Israel whom I have chosen.
2 Thus says Yahweh who made you,
who formed you in the womb;
  he will help you.
Do not be afraid, Jacob my servant,
Jeshurun whom I have chosen.
3 For I shall pour out water
  on the thirsty soil
and streams on the dry ground.
I shall pour out my spirit
  on your descendants,
my blessing on your offspring,
4 and they will spring up among the grass,

like willows on the banks of a stream.
5 One person will say, 'I belong to Yahweh,'
   another will call himself by Jacob's name.
   On his hand another will write 'Yahweh's'
   and be surnamed 'Israel'.

THERE IS ONLY ONE GOD

6 Thus says Yahweh, Israel's king,
   Yahweh Sabaoth, his redeemer:
   I am the first and I am the last;
   there is no God except me.
7 Who is like me? Let him call out,
   let him affirm it and convince me it is so;
   let him say what has been happening
   since I instituted an eternal people,
   and predict to them what will happen next!
8 Have no fear, do not be afraid:
   have I not told you
       and revealed it long ago?
   You are my witnesses.
   Is there any God except me?
   There is no Rock; I know of none.

THE FATUITY OF IDOLS

9The makers of idols are all nothingness; the works they
delight in serve no purpose. And these are the witness

against them: they see nothing, they know nothing; and so they will be put to shame. [10]Who ever fashioned a god or cast an image without hope of gain? [11]Watch how all its devotees will be put to shame, and the men who made it too, who are only human. Let them all assemble, let them stand forward and feel both fear and shame!

[12]The blacksmith makes an axe over the charcoal, beats it into shape with a hammer, works on it with his strong arm. Then he feels hungry and his strength deserts him; having drunk no water, he is exhausted.

[13]The wood carver[b] takes his measurements, outlines the image with chalk, executes it with the chisel, following the outline with a compass. He makes it look like a human being, with human standards of beauty, so that it can reside in a house. [14]He has cut down cedars, has selected an oak and a terebinth which he has grown for himself among the trees in the forest and has planted a pine tree which the rain has nourished. [15]Once it is suitable to burn, he takes some of it to warm himself; having kindled it, he bakes bread. But he also makes a god and worships it; he makes an idol from it and bows down before it. [16]Half of it he burns on the fire, over this half he roasts meat, eats it and is replete; at the same time he warms himself and says, 'Ah, how warm I am, watching the flames!' [17]With the remainder he makes a god, his idol, bows down before it, worships it and prays to it. 'Save me,' he says, 'for you are my god.'

[18]They know nothing, they understand nothing, since

their eyes are incapable of seeing and their hearts of reflecting. ¹⁹Not one of them looks into his heart, not one of them has the knowledge and wit to think, 'I burned half of it on the fire and cooked food over the embers. Am I right to make something disgusting out of what is left? Am I right to bow down before a block of wood?'

²⁰He hankers after ashes, his deluded heart has led him astray; he will not save himself, he will not think, 'What I have in my hand is nothing but a lie!'

LOYALTY TO YAHWEH

²¹ Remember these things, Jacob,
and Israel, since you are my servant.
I formed you, you are my servant;
Israel, I shall not forget you.
²² I have dispelled your acts of revolt
like a cloud
and your sins like a mist.
Come back to me,
for I have redeemed you.
²³ Heavens, shout for joy, for
Yahweh has acted!
Underworld, shout aloud!
Shout for joy, you mountains,
forests and all your trees!
For Yahweh has redeemed Jacob
and displayed his glory in Israel.

GOD, CREATOR OF THE WORLD AND LORD OF HISTORY

²⁴ Thus says Yahweh, your redeemer,
   he who formed you in the womb:
   I, Yahweh, have made all things,
   I alone spread out the heavens.
   When I hammered the earth into shape,
      who was with me?
²⁵ I, who foil the omens of soothsayers
   and make fools of diviners,
   who confound sages
   turning their knowledge into folly,
²⁶ who confirm the word of my servant
   and make the plans of my
   envoys succeed;
   who say to Jerusalem,
      'You will be inhabited,'
   and to the towns of Judah,
      'You will be rebuilt
   and I shall restore the ruins
      of Jerusalem';
²⁷ who say to the ocean, 'Dry up!
   I shall make your rivers run dry';
²⁸ who say to Cyrus, 'My shepherd.'
   He will perform my entire will
   by saying to Jerusalem,
      'You will be rebuilt,'

and to the Temple,
  'You will be refounded.'

CYRUS, THE INSTRUMENT OF GOD

45 Thus says Yahweh
to his anointed one,
to Cyrus whom, he says,
  I have grasped by his right hand,
to make the nations bow before him
and to disarm kings,
to open gateways before him
so that their gates be closed no more:

2 I myself shall go before you,
I shall level the heights,
I shall shatter the bronze gateways,
I shall smash the iron bars.

3 I shall give you secret treasures
and hidden hoards of wealth,
so that you will know that I am Yahweh,
who call you by your name,
the God of Israel.

4 It is for the sake of my servant Jacob
and of Israel my chosen one,
that I have called you by your name,
have given you a title
  though you do not know me.

5 I am Yahweh, and there is no other,

there is no other God except me.
Though you do not know me,
    I have armed you
6 so that it may be known from east to west
that there is no one except me.
I am Yahweh, and there is no other,
7 I form the light and I create the darkness,
I make well-being, and I create disaster,
I, Yahweh, do all these things.

PRAYER

8 Rain down, you heavens, from above,
and let the clouds pour down
    saving justice,
let the earth open up
    and blossom with salvation,
and let justice sprout with it;
I, Yahweh, have created it!

THE SUPREME POWER OF YAHWEH

9 Woe to anyone who argues with his Maker,
one earthenware pot among many!
Does the clay say to its potter,
    'What are you doing?
Your work has no hands!'
10 Woe to anyone who asks a father,

'Why are you begetting?'
and a woman, 'Why are you giving birth?'
11 Thus says Yahweh,
the Holy One of Israel and his Maker:
I am asked for signs regarding my sons,
I am given orders about the work I do.
12   It was I who made the earth
and I created human beings on it,
mine were the hands
that spread out the heavens
and I have given the orders
to all their array.
13 I myself have raised him in saving justice
and I shall make all paths level for him.
He will rebuild my city
and bring my exiles home
without ransom or indemnity,
says Yahweh Sabaoth.

THE CONVERSION OF THE NATIONS

14 Thus says Yahweh:
The produce of Egypt,
the commerce of Cush
and the men of Seba, tall of stature,
will come over to you and belong to you.
They will follow you, walking in chains,
they will bow before you,

they will pray to you,
'With you alone is God,
   and there is no other!
The gods do not exist.'

¹⁵ Truly, you are a God
   who conceals himself,
God of Israel, Saviour!

¹⁶ They are shamed and humbled,
   every one of them,
humiliated they go, the makers of idols.

¹⁷ Israel will be saved by Yahweh,
saved everlastingly.
You will never be ashamed or humiliated
for ever and ever.

¹⁸ For thus says Yahweh,
   the Creator of the heavens—
he is God, who shaped the earth
   and made it,
who set it firm;
he did not create it to be chaos,
he formed it to be lived in:
I am Yahweh, and there is no other.

¹⁹ I have not spoken in secret,
in some dark corner of the underworld.
I did not say, 'Offspring of Jacob,
search for me in chaos!'
I am Yahweh: I proclaim saving justice,
I say what is true.

GOD, LORD OF THE WHOLE UNIVERSE

[20] Assemble, come,
all of you gather round,
survivors of the nations.
They have no knowledge,
those who parade their wooden idols
and pray to a god
that cannot save.

[21] Speak up, present your case,
let them put their heads together!
Who foretold this in the past,
who revealed it long ago?
Was it not I, Yahweh?
There is no other god except me,
no saving God, no Saviour except me!

[22] Turn to me and you will be saved,
all you ends of the earth,
for I am God, and there is no other.

[23] By my own self I swear it;
what comes from my mouth
is saving justice,
it is an irrevocable word:
All shall bend the knee to me,
by me every tongue shall swear,

[24] saying, 'In Yahweh alone
are saving justice and strength,'
until all those who used to rage at him

come to him in shame.
25 In Yahweh the whole race of Israel
finds justice and glory.

THE FALL OF BABYLON

46 Bel is crouching, Nebo cowering,
their idols are being put on animals,
on beasts of burden,
the loads you have been carrying
are a burden to a weary beast.
2 They are cowering
     and crouching together,
no one can save this burden,
they themselves have gone into captivity.
3 Listen to me, House of Jacob,
all who remain of the House of Israel,
whom I have carried since the womb,
whom I have supported
     since you were conceived.
4 Until your old age I shall be the same,
until your hair is grey I shall carry you.
As I have done, so I shall support you,
I myself shall carry and shall save you.
5 With whom can you compare me,
     equate me,
to whom can you liken me,
     making equals of us?

⁶ They lavish gold from their purses
and weigh out silver on the scales.
They engage a goldsmith to make a god,
then bow low and actually adore!

⁷ They lift it on their shoulders and carry it,
and put it down where it is meant to stand,
so that it never moves from the spot.
You may cry out to it in distress,
it never replies,
it never saves anyone in trouble.

⁸ Remember this and stand firm;
rebels, look into your hearts.

⁹ Remember the things
that happened long ago,
for I am God, and there is no other;
I am God, and there is none like me.

¹⁰ From the beginning I revealed the future,
in advance, what has not yet occurred.
I say: My purpose will come about,
I shall do whatever I please;

¹¹ I call a bird of prey from the east,
my man predestined, from a distant land.
What I have said, I shall do,
what I have planned, I shall perform.

¹² Listen to me, you hard-hearted people
far removed from saving justice:

¹³ I am bringing my justice nearer,
it is not far away,

my salvation will not delay.
I shall place my salvation in Zion
and my glory in Israel.

LAMENT FOR BABYLON

47 Step down! Sit in the dust,
virgin daughter of Babylon.
Sit on the ground, no throne,
daughter of the Chaldaeans,
for never again will you be called
tender and delicate.
2 Take the grinding mill, crush up the meal.
Remove your veil,
tie up your skirt, bare your legs,
cross the rivers.
3 Let your nakedness be displayed
and your shame exposed.
I am going to take vengeance
and no one will stand in my way.

4 Our redeemer,
Yahweh Sabaoth is his name,
the Holy One of Israel, says:
5 Sit in silence, bury yourself in darkness,
daughter of the Chaldaeans,
for never again will you be called
the mistress of kingdoms.

⁶ Being angry with my people,
   I rejected my heritage,
   surrendering them into your clutches.
   You showed them no mercy,
   you made your yoke very heavy
      on the aged.
⁷ You thought, 'I shall be a queen for ever.'
   You did not reflect on these matters
   or think about the future.

⁸ Now listen to this, voluptuous woman,
   lolling at ease
   and thinking to yourself,
   'I am the only one who matters.
   I shall never be widowed,
   never know bereavement.'
⁹ Yet both these things will befall you,
   suddenly, in one day.
   Bereavement and widowhood
   will suddenly befall you
   in spite of all your witchcraft
   and the potency of your spells.
¹⁰ Confident in your wickedness,
   you thought, 'No one can see me.'
   Your wishes and your knowledge
   were what deluded you,
   as you thought to yourself,
   'I am the only one who matters.'

¹¹ Hence, disaster will befall you
which you will not know
how to charm away,
calamity overtake you
which you will not be able to avert,
ruination will suddenly befall you,
such as you have never known.

¹² Keep to your spells then,
and all your sorceries,
at which you have worked so hard
since you were young.
Perhaps you will succeed,
perhaps you will strike terror!

¹³ You have had many tiring consultations:
let the astrologers come forward now
and save you,
the star-gazers
who announce month by month
what will happen to you next.

¹⁴ Look, they are like wisps of straw,
the fire will burn them up.
They will not save their lives
from the power of the flame.
No embers these, for keeping warm,
no fire to sit beside!

¹⁵ Such will your wizards prove to be for you,
for whom you have worked so hard
since you were young;

each wandering his own way,
none of them can save you.

YAHWEH HAS FORETOLD EVERYTHING

48 Listen to this, House of Jacob,
you who are called by the name of Israel
and issued from the waters of Judah,
who swear by the name of Yahweh
and invoke the God of Israel,
though not in good faith or uprightness;

2 for they call themselves after the holy city
and rely on the God of Israel,
Yahweh Sabaoth is his name.

3 Things now past I revealed long ago,
they issued from my mouth,
    I proclaimed them;
suddenly I acted and they happened.

4 For I knew you to be obstinate,
your neck an iron sinew
and your forehead bronze.

5 As I told you about it long before,
before it happened I revealed it to you,
so that you could not say,
    'My statue did it,
my idol, my metal image, ordained this.'

6 You have heard and seen all this,

why won't you admit it?
Now I am going to reveal
   new things to you,
secrets that you do not know;

7 they have just been created, not long ago,
and until today you have heard
   nothing about them,
so that you cannot say,
   'Yes, I knew about this.'

8 No, you have not heard,
   you have not known,
for a long time your ear
   has not been attentive,
for I knew how treacherous you were;
you have been called a rebel
   since the womb.

9 For the sake of my name
   I shall defer my anger,
for the sake of my honour
   I shall be patient with you,
     rather than destroy you.

10 Look I have purchased you,
   but not for silver,
I have chosen you
   out of the cauldron of affliction.

11 For my sake and my sake only shall I act,
for why should my name be profaned?
I will not yield my glory to another.

YAHWEH HAS CHOSEN CYRUS

¹² Listen to me, Jacob,
   Israel whom I have called:
   I, and none else, am the first,
   I am also the last.
¹³ My hand laid the foundations of earth
   and my right hand spread out the heavens.
   I summon them
   and they all present themselves together.
¹⁴ Assemble, all of you, and listen;
   which of them has revealed this?
   Yahweh loves him; he will do his pleasure
   on Babylon and the race of the Chaldaeans;
¹⁵ I, I have spoken,
   yes, I have summoned him, I have brought him,
   and he will succeed.

ISRAEL'S DESTINY

¹⁶ Come near and listen to this:
   from the first, I never spoke obscurely;
   when it happened, I was there,
   and now Lord Yahweh has sent me
      with his spirit.
¹⁷ Thus says Yahweh, your redeemer,
      the Holy One of Israel:
   I am Yahweh your God

and teach you for your own good,
I lead you in the way you ought to go.

¹⁸ If only you had listened
to my commandments!
Your prosperity would have been
like a river
and your saving justice
like the waves of the sea.

¹⁹ Your descendants would have been
numbered like the sand,
your offspring as many as its grains.
Their name would never be cancelled
or blotted out from my presence.

THE END OF THE EXILE

²⁰ Come out from Babylon!
Flee from the Chaldaeans!
Declare this with cries of joy,
proclaim it,
carry it to the remotest parts of earth,
say, 'Yahweh has redeemed
his servant Jacob.'

²¹ Those he led through the arid country
never went thirsty;
he made water flow for them
from the rock,
he split the rock

and out streamed the water.

22 There is no peace, says Yahweh,
for the wicked.

SECOND SONG OF THE SERVANT

49 Coasts and islands, listen to me,
pay attention, distant peoples.
Yahweh called me when I was in the womb,
before my birth
he had pronounced my name.

2 He made my mouth like a sharp sword,
he hid me in the shadow of his hand.
He made me into a sharpened arrow
and concealed me in his quiver.

3 He said to me, 'Israel, you are my servant,
through whom I shall manifest my glory.'

4 But I said, 'My toil has been futile,
I have exhausted myself for nothing,
to no purpose.'
Yet all the while
my cause was with Yahweh
and my reward with my God.

5 And now Yahweh has spoken,
who formed me in the womb
to be his servant,
to bring Jacob back to him
and to re-unite Israel to him;

—I shall be honoured in Yahweh's eyes,
and my God has been my strength. —

6 He said, 'It is not enough for you
to be my servant,
to restore the tribes of Jacob
and bring back the survivors of Israel;
I shall make you a light to the nations
so that my salvation may reach
the remotest parts of earth.'

7 Thus says Yahweh,
the redeemer, the Holy One of Israel,
to the one who is despised,
detested by the nation,
to the slave of despots:
Kings will stand up when they see,
princes will see and bow low,
because of Yahweh who is faithful,
the Holy One of Israel
who has chosen you.

THE JOYFUL HOMECOMING

8 Thus says Yahweh:
At the time of my favour
I have answered you,
on the day of salvation I have helped you.
I have formed you and have appointed you
to be the covenant for a people,

    to restore the land,
    to return ravaged properties,
⁹ to say to prisoners, 'Come out,'
    to those who are in darkness,
        'Show yourselves.'
    Along the roadway they will graze,
    and any bare height will be their pasture.
¹⁰ They will never hunger or thirst,
    scorching wind and sun
        will never plague them;
    for he who pities them will lead them,
    will guide them to springs of water.
¹¹ I shall turn all my mountains into a road
    and my highways will be raised aloft.
¹² Look! Here they come from far away,
    look, these from the north and the west,
    those from the land of Sinim.

¹³ Shout for joy, you heavens; earth, exult!
    Mountains, break into joyful cries!
    For Yahweh has consoled his people,
    is taking pity on his afflicted ones.
¹⁴ Zion was saying,
        'Yahweh has abandoned me,
    the Lord has forgotten me.'
¹⁵ Can a woman forget her baby at the breast,
    feel no pity for the child she has borne?
    Even if these were to forget,

I shall not forget you.
¹⁶ Look, I have engraved you
    on the palms of my hands,
your ramparts are ever before me.
¹⁷ Your rebuilders are hurrying,
your destroyers and despoilers
    will soon go away.

¹⁸ Raise your eyes and look around you:
all are assembling, coming to you.
By my life, declares Yahweh,
you will put them all on like jewels,
like a bride, you will fasten them on.
¹⁹ For your desolate places and your ruins
and your devastated country
from now on will be too cramped
    for your inhabitants,
and your devourers will be far away.
²⁰ Once more they will say in your hearing,
the children of whom you were bereft,
'The place is too cramped for me,
make room for me to live.'
²¹ Then you will think to yourself,
'Who has borne me these?
I was bereft and barren,
exiled, turned out of my home;
who has reared these?
I was left all alone,

so where have these come from?'

²² Thus says Lord Yahweh:
Look, I am beckoning to the nations
and hoisting a signal to the peoples:
they will bring your sons in their arms
and your daughters will be carried
    on their shoulders.
²³ Kings will be your foster-fathers
and their princesses, your foster-mothers.
They will fall prostrate before you,
    faces to the ground,
and lick the dust at your feet.
And you will know that I am Yahweh;
those who hope in me
    will not be disappointed.
²⁴ Can the body be snatched from the warrior,
can the tyrant's captive be set free?
²⁵ But thus says Yahweh:
The warrior's captive
    will indeed be snatched away
and the tyrant's booty
    will indeed be set free;
I myself shall fight those who fight you
and I myself shall save your children.
²⁶ I shall make your oppressors
    eat their own flesh,
they will be as drunk on their own blood

as on new wine.
And all humanity will know
that I am Yahweh, your Saviour,
your redeemer, the Mighty One of Jacob.

ISRAEL'S PUNISHMENT

50 Thus says Yahweh:
Where is your mother's writ of divorce
by which I repudiated her?
Or to which of my creditors
have I sold you?
Look, you have been sold
for your own misdeeds,
your mother was repudiated
for your acts of rebellion.
2 Why was there no one there when I came?
Why did no one answer when I called?
Is my hand too short to redeem?
Have I not strength to save?
Look, with a threat I can dry the sea,
and turn rivers to desert;
the fish in them go rotten for want of water
and die of thirst.
3 I dress the heavens in black,
I cover them in sackcloth.

THIRD SONG OF THE SERVANT

⁴ Lord Yahweh has given me
    a disciple's tongue,
for me to know how to give
    a word of comfort to the weary.
Morning by morning
    he makes my ear alert
to listen like a disciple.
⁵ Lord Yahweh has opened my ear
and I have not resisted,
I have not turned away.
⁶ I have offered my back
    to those who struck me,
my cheeks to those
    who plucked my beard;
I have not turned my face away
from insult and spitting.
⁷ Lord Yahweh comes to my help,
this is why insult has not touched me,
this is why I have set my face like flint
and know that I shall not
    be put to shame.
⁸ He who grants me saving justice is near!
Who will bring a case against me?
Let us appear in court together!
Who has a case against me?
Let him approach me!

⁹ Look, Lord Yahweh is coming
        to my help!
    Who dares condemn me?
    Look at them, all falling apart
    like moth-eaten clothes!

¹⁰ Which of you fears Yahweh
    and listens to his servant's voice?
    Which of you walks in darkness
    and sees no light?
    Let him trust in the name of Yahweh
    and lean on his God!

¹¹ Look, all you who light a fire
    and arm yourselves with firebrands,
    walk by the light of your fire
    and the firebrands you have kindled!
    This is what you will get from me:
    you will lie down in torment!

THE BLESSINGS IN STORE FOR THE CHOSEN PEOPLE

51 Listen to me,
        you who pursue saving justice,
    you who seek Yahweh.
    Consider the rock
        from which you were hewn,
    the quarry from which you were dug.

² Consider Abraham your father

and Sarah who gave you birth.
When I called him he was the only one
but I blessed him and made him numerous.
³ Yes, Yahweh has pity on Zion,
has pity on all her ruins;
he will turn her desert into an Eden
and her wastelands
into the garden of Yahweh.
Joy and gladness will be found in her,
thanksgiving and the sound of music.

GOD'S REIGN OF SAVING JUSTICE

⁴ Pay attention to me, my people,
listen to me, my nation,
for a law will come from me,
and I shall make my saving justice
the light of peoples.
⁵ My justice is suddenly approaching,
my salvation appears,
my arm is about to judge the peoples.
The coasts and islands
will put their hope in me
and put their trust in my arm.
⁶ Raise your eyes to the heavens,
look down at the earth;
for the heavens will vanish like smoke,
the earth wear out like clothing

and its inhabitants die like vermin,
but my salvation will last for ever
and my saving justice remain inviolable.

7 Listen to me, you who know
what saving justice means,
a people who take my laws to heart:
do not fear people's taunts,
do not be alarmed by their insults,
8 for the moth will eat them like clothing,
the grub will devour them like wool,
but my saving justice will last for ever
and my salvation for all generations.

THE AWAKENING OF YAHWEH

9 Awake, awake!
Clothe yourself in strength,
arm of Yahweh.
Awake, as in the olden days,
generations long ago!
Was it not you who split Rahab[22] in half,
who pierced the Dragon through?
10 Was it not you who dried up the sea,
the waters of the great Abyss;
who made the sea-bed into a road
for the redeemed to go across?
11 This is why

those whom Yahweh has ransomed
will return,
they will enter Zion shouting for joy,
their heads crowned with a joy unending;
joy and gladness will escort them
and sorrow and sighing will take flight.

YAHWEH, THE CONSOLER

¹² I, I am your consoler.
Why then should you be afraid
of mortal human beings
of a child of man,
whose fate is that of the grass?
¹³ You forget about Yahweh your Creator
who spread out the heavens
and laid the earth's foundations;
you have never stopped trembling
all day long
before the fury of the oppressor
when he was bent on destruction.
Where is the oppressor's fury now?
¹⁴ The despairing captive
is soon to be set free;
he will not die in the dungeon,
nor will his food run out.
¹⁵ I am Yahweh your God
who stirs up the sea,

> making its waves roar—
> Yahweh Sabaoth is my name.

[16] I put my words into your mouth,
> I hid you in the shadow of my hand,
> to spread out the heavens
>   and lay the earth's foundations
> and say to Zion, 'You are my people.'

THE AWAKENING OF JERUSALEM

[17] Awake, awake!
> To your feet, Jerusalem!
> You who from Yahweh's hand
> have drunk the cup of his wrath.
> The chalice, the stupefying cup,
> you have drained to the dregs.

[18] There is no one to guide her
> of all the children she has borne,
> no one to grasp her hand
> of all the children she has reared.

[19] Double disaster has befallen you—
> who is there to sympathise?
> Pillage and ruin, famine and sword—
> who is there to console you?

[20] Your children are lying helpless
> at the end of every street
> like an antelope trapped in a net;
> they are filled to the brim

with Yahweh's wrath,
with the rebuke of your God.
²¹ So listen to this, afflicted one,
drunk, though not with wine.
²² Thus says your Lord Yahweh,
your God, defender of your people:
Look, I am taking
the stupefying cup from your hand,
the chalice, the cup of my wrath,
you will not have to drink again.
²³ I shall hand it to your tormentors
who used to say to you,
'On the ground!
So that we can walk over you!'
And you would flatten your back
like the ground,
like a street for them to walk on.

THE LIBERATION OF JERUSALEM

52 Awake, awake!
Clothe yourself in strength, Zion.
Put on your finest clothes,
Jerusalem, Holy City;
for the uncircumcised and the unclean
will enter you no more.
² Shake off your dust; get up,
captive Jerusalem!

The chains have fallen from your neck,
captive daughter of Jerusalem!

3 For Yahweh says this,
'You were sold for nothing;
you will be redeemed without money.'
4 For the Lord Yahweh says this,
'Long ago my people went to Egypt
and settled there as aliens;
finally Assyria oppressed them
for no reason.
5 So now what is to be done,'
declares Yahweh,
'since my people have been carried off
for nothing,
their masters howl in triumph,'
declares Yahweh,
'and my name is held in contempt
all day, every day?
6 Because of this
my people will know my name,
because of this
they will know when the day comes,
that it is I saying, Here I am!'

A PREDICTION OF SALVATION

7 How beautiful on the mountains,
   are the feet of the messenger
      announcing peace,
   of the messenger of good news,
   who proclaims salvation
   and says to Zion,
   'Your God is king!'
8 The voices of your watchmen!
   Now they raise their voices,
   shouting for joy together,
   for with their own eyes they have seen
   Yahweh returning to Zion.
9 Break into shouts together,
   shouts of joy, you ruins of Jerusalem;
   for Yahweh has consoled his people,
   he has redeemed Jerusalem.
10 Yahweh has bared his holy arm
   for all the nations to see,
   and all the ends of the earth
   have seen the salvation of our God.
11 Go away, go away, leave that place,
   do not touch anything unclean.
   Get out of her, purify yourselves
   you who carry Yahweh's vessels!
12 For you are not to hurry away,
   you are not to leave like fugitives.

No, Yahweh marches at your head
and the God of Israel is your rearguard.

FOURTH SONG OF THE SERVANT

¹³ Look, my servant will prosper,
   will grow great, will rise to great heights.
¹⁴ As many people were aghast at him
   —he was so inhumanly disfigured
   that he no longer looked like a man—
¹⁵ so many nations will be astonished
   and kings will stay tight-lipped
   before him,
   seeing what had never been told them,
   learning what they had not heard before.

53 Who has given credence
   to what we have heard?
   And who has seen in it
      a revelation of Yahweh's arm?
² Like a sapling he grew up before him,
   like a root in arid ground.
   He had no form or charm to attract us,
   no beauty to win our hearts;
³ he was despised, the lowest of men,
   a man of sorrows, familiar with suffering,
   one from whom, as it were,
      we averted our gaze,
   despised, for whom we had no regard.

4 Yet ours were the sufferings
   he was bearing,
ours the sorrows he was carrying,
while we thought of him
   as someone being punished
and struck with affliction by God;

5 whereas he was being wounded
   for our rebellions,
crushed because of our guilt;
the punishment reconciling us fell on him,
and we have been healed by his bruises.

6 We had all gone astray like sheep,
each taking his own way,
and Yahweh brought the acts of rebellion
of all of us to bear on him.

7 Ill-treated and afflicted,
he never opened his mouth,
like a lamb led to the slaughter-house,
like a sheep dumb before its shearers
he never opened his mouth.

8 Forcibly, after sentence, he was taken.
Which of his contemporaries
   was concerned
at his having been cut off
   from the land of the living,
at his having been struck dead
   for his people's rebellion?

9 He was given a grave with the wicked,
   and his tomb is with the rich,
   although he had done no violence,
   had spoken no deceit.

10 It was Yahweh's good pleasure
   to crush him with pain;
   if he gives his life as a sin offering,
   he will see his offspring
     and prolong his life,
   and through him
     Yahweh's good pleasure will be done.

11 After the ordeal he has endured,
   he will see the light and be content.
   By his knowledge, the upright one,
     my servant will justify many
   by taking their guilt on himself.

12 Hence I shall give him a portion
     with the many,
   and he will share the booty
     with the mighty,
   for having exposed himself to death
   and for being counted
     as one of the rebellious,
   whereas he was bearing the sin of many
   and interceding for the rebellious.

JERUSALEM RESTORED TO YAHWEH'S FAVOUR

54 Shout for joy, barren one
who has borne no children!
Break into cries and shouts of joy,
    you who were never in labour!
For the children of the forsaken one
    are more in number
than the children of the wedded wife,
    says Yahweh.

2 Widen the space of your tent
extend the curtains of your home,
    do not hold back!
Lengthen your ropes,
    make your tent-pegs firm,

3 for you will burst out to right and to left,
your race will dispossess the nations
and repopulate deserted towns.

4 Do not fear,
    you will not be put to shame again
do not worry,
    you will not be disgraced again;
for you will forget the shame of your youth
and no longer remember
    he dishonour of your widowhood.

5 For your Creator is your husband,
Yahweh Sabaoth is his name,

the Holy One of Israel is your redeemer,
he is called God of the whole world.

6 Yes, Yahweh has called you back
like a forsaken, grief-stricken wife,
like the repudiated wife of his youth,
says your God.

7 I did forsake you for a brief moment,
but in great compassion
    I shall take you back.

8 In a flood of anger, for a moment
I hid my face from you.
But in everlasting love
    I have taken pity on you,
says Yahweh, your redeemer.

9 For me it will be as in the days of Noah
when I swore that Noah's waters
should never flood the world again.
So now I swear never to be angry with you
and never to rebuke you again.

10 For the mountains may go away
and the hills may totter,
but my faithful love will never leave you,
my covenant of peace will never totter,
says Yahweh who takes pity on you.

THE NEW JERUSALEM

11 Unhappy creature, storm-tossed,
      unpitied,
  look, I shall lay your stones on agates
  and your foundations on sapphires.
12 I shall make your battlements rubies,
  your gateways firestone
  and your entire wall precious stones.
13 All your children
      will be taught by Yahweh
  and great will be
      your children's prosperity.
14 In saving justice you will be made firm,
  free from oppression:
      you will have nothing to fear;
  free from terror:
      it will not approach you.
15 Should anyone attack you,
      that will not be my doing,
  and whoever does attack you,
      for your sake will fall.
16 I created the smith
  who blows on the charcoal-fire
  to produce a weapon for his use;
  I also created the destroyer
  to ruin it.
17 No weapon forged against you

will succeed.
Any voice raised against you in court
    you will refute.
Such is the lot
    of the servants of Yahweh,
the saving justice I assure them,
declares Yahweh.

FINAL INVITATION

55 Oh, come to the water
    all you who are thirsty;
though you have no money, come!
Buy and eat; come, buy wine and milk
without money, free!
² Why spend money on what cannot nourish
and your wages on what fails to satisfy?
Listen carefully to me,
    and you will have good things to eat
    and rich food to enjoy.
³ Pay attention, come to me;
    listen, and you will live.

I shall make an everlasting covenant
    with you
in fulfilment of the favours
    promised to David.

⁴ Look, I have made him a witness
      to peoples,
   a leader and lawgiver to peoples.
⁵ Look, you will summon a nation
      unknown to you,
   a nation unknown to you will hurry to you
   for the sake of Yahweh your God,
   because the Holy One of Israel
      has glorified you.

⁶ Seek out Yahweh
      while he is still to be found,
   call to him while he is still near.
⁷ Let the wicked abandon his way
   and the evil one his thoughts.
   Let him turn back to Yahweh
      who will take pity on him,
   to our God, for he is rich in forgiveness;
⁸ for my thoughts are not your thoughts
   and your ways are not my ways,
   declares Yahweh.
⁹ For the heavens are as high above earth
   as my ways are above your ways,
   my thoughts above your thoughts.
¹⁰ For, as the rain and the snow
      come down from the sky
   and do not return
      before having watered the earth,

fertilising it and making it germinate
to provide seed for the sower
and food to eat,
¹¹ so it is with the word
that goes from my mouth:
it will not return to me unfulfilled
or before having carried out
my good pleasure
and having achieved
what it was sent to do.

CONCLUSION

¹² Yes, you will go out with joy
and be led away in safety.
Mountains and hills
will break into joyful cries before you
and all the trees of the countryside
clap their hands.
¹³ Cypress will grow instead of thorns,
myrtle instead of nettles.
And this will be fame for Yahweh,
an eternal monument
never to be effaced.

THE THIRD PART OF THE BOOK OF ISAIAH

PROMISES TO FOREIGNERS

56 Thus says Yahweh:
Make fair judgement your concern,
    act with justice,
for soon my salvation will come
and my saving justice be manifest.

2 Blessed is anyone who does this,
anyone who clings to it,
observing the Sabbath, not profaning it,
and abstaining from every evil deed.

3 No foreigner adhering to Yahweh
        should say,
'Yahweh will utterly exclude me
        from his people.'
No eunuch should say,
'Look, I am a dried-up tree.'

4 For Yahweh says this:
    To the eunuchs
        who observe my Sabbaths
and choose to do my good pleasure
and cling to my covenant,

⁵ I shall give them in my house
        and within my walls
a monument and a name
        better than sons and daughters;
I shall give them an everlasting name
that will never be effaced.
⁶ As for foreigners
        who adhere to Yahweh to serve him
to love Yahweh's name
        and become his servants,
all who observe the Sabbath,
        not profaning it,
and cling to my covenant:
⁷ these I shall lead to my holy mountain
and make them joyful
        in my house of prayer.
Their burnt offerings and sacrifices
        will be accepted on my altar,
for my house will be called
        a house of prayer for all peoples.

⁸ Lord Yahweh
        who gathers the exiles of Israel declares:
There are others I shall gather
        besides those already gathered.
⁹ Come and gorge, all you wild beasts,
all you beasts of the forest!

THE UNWORTHINESS OF THE NATION'S LEADERS

¹⁰ Its watchmen are all blind,
they know nothing.
Dumb watchdogs all, unable to bark,
they dream, lie down, and love to sleep.
¹¹ Greedy dogs, never satisfied,
such are the shepherds,
who understand nothing;
they all go their own way,
each to the last man after his own interest.
¹² 'Come, let me fetch wine;
we will get drunk on strong drink,
tomorrow will be just as wonderful
as today
and even more so!'

57 The upright person perishes
and no one cares.
The faithful is taken off
and no one takes it to heart.
Yes, because of the evil times
the upright is taken off;
² he will enter peace,
and those who follow the right way
will find rest on their beds.

AGAINST IDOLATRY

³ But you, you children of a witch,
    come here,
adulterous race prostituting yourselves!

⁴ At whom are you jeering,
at whom are you making faces
and sticking out your tongue?
Are you not the spawn of rebellion,
a lying race?

⁵ Lusting among the terebinths,
and under every spreading tree,
sacrificing children in the ravines,
below the clefts in the rocks.

⁶ The smooth stones of the ravines
    will be your portion,
yes, these will be your lot.
To these you have poured libations,
have brought your cereal offering.
Can all this appease me?

⁷ On a mountain high and lofty
you have put your bed.
Thither, too, you have climbed
to offer sacrifice.

⁸ Behind door and doorpost
you have set your reminder.
Yes, far from me, you exposed yourself,

climbed on to your bed,
and made the most of it.
You struck a profitable bargain
with those whose bed you love,
whoring with them often,
with your eyes on the sacred symbol.

9 You went to Molech with oil,
you were prodigal with your perfumes;
you sent your envoys far afield,
down to Sheol itself.

10 Though tired by so much travelling,
you never said, 'It is no use.'
Finding your strength revive,
you never gave up.

11 Who was it you dreaded, and feared,
that you should betray me,
no longer remember me
and not spare a thought for me?
Was I not silent for a long time?
So you cannot have been afraid of me.

12 Now I shall expose
this uprightness of yours,
and little good it did you.

13 When you cry for help,
let those thronging round you save you!
The wind will carry them all away,
one puff will take them off.
But whoever trusts in me

will inherit the country,
he will own my holy mountain.

SALVATION FOR THE WEAK

¹⁴ Then it will be said:
Level up, level up, clear the way,
remove the obstacle
    from my people's way,
¹⁵ for thus says the High and Exalted One
who lives eternally
and whose name is holy,
'I live in the holy heights
but I am with the contrite and humble
to revive the spirit of the humble,
to revive the heart of the contrite.

¹⁶ 'For I do not want to be forever accusing
nor always to be angry,
or the spirit would fail
    under my onslaught,
the souls that I myself have made.

¹⁷ 'Angered by his wicked cupidity,
I hid and struck him in anger,
but he rebelliously went the way
    of his choice.

¹⁸ 'I saw how he behaved,
      but I shall heal him,
   I shall lead him,
      fill him with consolation,
   him and those who mourn for him,
¹⁹ bringing praise to their lips.
   Peace, peace to far and near,
      Yahweh says,
   and I shall heal him.'
²⁰ The wicked, however,
      are like the restless sea
   that cannot be still,
   whose waters throw up mud and dirt.
²¹ 'No peace', says Yahweh,
      'for the wicked.'

FASTING PLEASING TO GOD

58 Shout for all you are worth,
   do not hold back,
   raise your voice like a trumpet.
   To my people
      proclaim their rebellious acts,
   to the House of Jacob, their sins.
² They seek for me day after day,
   they long to know my ways,
   like a nation that has acted uprightly
   and not forsaken the law of its God.

They ask me for laws that are upright,
they long to be near God:

3 'Why have we fasted, if you do not see,
why mortify ourselves if you never notice?'
Look, you seek your own pleasure
     on your fastdays
and you exploit all your workmen;

4 look, the only purpose of your fasting
     is to quarrel and squabble
and strike viciously with your fist.
Fasting like yours today
will never make your voice heard on high.

5 Is that the sort of fast that pleases me,
a day when a person
     inflicts pain on himself?
Hanging your head like a reed,
spreading out sackcloth and ashes?
Is that what you call fasting,
a day acceptable to Yahweh?

6 Is not this the sort of fast that pleases me:
to break unjust fetters,
to undo the thongs of the yoke,
to let the oppressed go free,
and to break all yokes?

7 Is it not sharing your food with the hungry,
and sheltering the homeless poor;
if you see someone lacking clothes,
     to clothe him,

and not to turn away from your own kin?

8 Then your light will blaze out
  like the dawn
and your wound be quickly healed over.
Saving justice will go ahead of you
and Yahweh's glory come behind you.

9 Then you will cry for help
  and Yahweh will answer;
you will call and he will say, 'I am here.'
If you do away with the yoke,
the clenched fist and malicious words,

10 if you deprive yourself for the hungry
and satisfy the needs of the afflicted,
your light will rise in the darkness,
and your darkest hour will be like noon.

11 Yahweh will always guide you,
will satisfy your needs
  in the scorched land;
he will give strength to your bones
and you will be like a watered garden,
like a flowing spring
whose waters never run dry.

12 Your ancient ruins will be rebuilt;
you will build on age-old foundations.
You will be called 'Breach-mender',
'Restorer of streets to be lived in'.

THE SABBATH

¹³ If you refrain
>   from breaking the Sabbath,
> from taking your own pleasure
>   on my holy day,
> if you call the Sabbath 'Delightful',
> and the day sacred to Yahweh
>   'Honourable',
> if you honour it
>   by abstaining from travel,
> from seeking your own pleasure
>   and from too much talk,
¹⁴ then you will find true happiness
>   in Yahweh,
> and I shall lead you in triumph
>   over the heights of the land.
> I shall feed you on the heritage
>   of your father Jacob,
> for the mouth of Yahweh has spoken.

PENITENTIAL PSALM

59 the arm of Yahweh
>   is not too short to save,
> nor his ear too dull to hear,
² but your guilty deeds have made a gulf
> between you and your God.

Your sins have made him
   hide his face from you
so as not to hear you,

3 since your hands are stained with blood
and your fingers with guilt;
your lips utter lies,
your tongues murmur wickedness.

4 No one makes upright accusations
or pleads sincerely.
All rely on empty words, utter falsehood,
conceive trouble and give birth to evil.

5 They are hatching adders' eggs
and weaving a spider's web;
eat one of their eggs and you die,
crush one and a viper emerges.

6 Their webs are useless for clothing,
their deeds are useless for wearing;
their deeds are deeds of guilt,
violence fills their hands.

7 Their feet run to do evil;
they are quick to shed innocent blood.
Their thoughts are thoughts of guilt,
wherever they go there is havoc and ruin.

8 They do not know the way of peace,
there is no fair judgement in their course,
they have made their own crooked paths,
and no one treading them knows any peace.

⁹ Thus fair judgement is remote from us
  nor can uprightness overtake us.
  We looked for light and all is darkness,
  for brightness and we walk in gloom.
¹⁰ Like the blind we feel our way along walls,
  we grope our way like people without eyes.
  We stumble as though noon were twilight,
  among the robust we are like the dead.
¹¹ We growl, all of us, like bears,
  like doves we make no sound but moaning,
  waiting for the fair judgement
      that never comes,
  for salvation, but that is far away.

¹² How often we have rebelled against you
  and our sins bear witness against us.
  Our rebellious acts are indeed with us,
  we are well aware of our guilt:
¹³ rebellion and denial of Yahweh,
  turning our back on our God,
  talking violence and revolt,
  murmuring lies in our heart.
¹⁴ Fair judgement is driven away
  and saving justice stands aloof,
  for good faith has stumbled in the street
  and sincerity cannot enter.
¹⁵ Good faith has vanished;
  anyone abstaining from evil is victimised.

Yahweh saw this and was displeased
that there was no fair judgement.
¹⁶ He saw there was no one
and wondered there was no one
    to intervene.
So he made his own arm his mainstay,
his own saving justice his support.
¹⁷ He put on saving justice like a breastplate,
on his head the helmet of salvation.
He put on the clothes of vengeance
    like a tunic
and wrapped himself in jealousy
    like a cloak.
¹⁸ To each he repays his due,
retribution to his enemies,
    reprisals on his foes,
to the coasts and islands
    he will repay their due.
¹⁹ From the west,
    Yahweh's name will be feared,
and from the east, his glory,
for he will come like a pent-up stream
impelled by the breath of Yahweh.
²⁰ Then for Zion will come a redeemer,
for those who stop rebelling in Jacob,
declares Yahweh.

PROPHECY

²¹'For my part, this is my covenant with them, says Yahweh. My spirit with which I endowed you, and my words that I have put in your mouth, will not leave your mouth, or the mouths of your children, or the mouths of your children's children, says Yahweh, henceforth and for ever.'

THE SPLENDOUR OF JERUSALEM

60 Arise, shine out,
for your light has come,
and the glory of Yahweh has risen on you.
² Look! though night still covers the earth
and darkness the peoples,
on you Yahweh is rising
and over you his glory can be seen.
³ The nations will come to your light
and kings to your dawning brightness.
⁴ Lift up your eyes and look around:
all are assembling
and coming towards you,
your sons coming from far away
and your daughters
being carried on the hip.
⁵ At this sight you will grow radiant,
your heart will throb and dilate,
since the riches of the sea will flow to you,

the wealth of the nations come to you;

6 camels in throngs will fill your streets,
the young camels of Midian and Ephah;
everyone in Saba will come,
bringing gold and incense
and proclaiming Yahweh's praises.

7 All the flocks of Kedar
will gather inside you,
the rams of Nebaioth will be at your service
as acceptable victims on my altar,
and I shall glorify my glorious house.

8 Who are these flying like a cloud,
like doves to their dovecote?

9 Why, the coasts and islands
put their hope in me
and the vessels of Tarshish take the lead
in bringing your children from far away,
and their silver and gold with them,
for the sake of the name of Yahweh
your God,
of the Holy One of Israel
who has made you glorious.

10 Foreigners will rebuild your walls
and their kings will serve you.
For though I struck you in anger,
in mercy I have pitied you.

11 Your gates will always be open,

never closed, either day or night,
for the riches of the nations
    to be brought you
and their kings to be let in.

12 For the nation and kingdom
    that will not serve you will perish,
and the nations will be utterly destroyed.

13 The glory of the Lebanon
    will come to you,
cypress, plane-tree, box-tree, one and all,
to adorn the site of my sanctuary,
for me to honour the place where I stand.

14 Your oppressors' children
    will numbly approach you,
at your feet all who despised you will fall
addressing you as 'City of Yahweh',
'Zion of the Holy One of Israel'.

15 Instead of your being forsaken and hated,
    avoided by everyone,
I will make you an object of eternal pride,
a source of joy from age to age.

16 You will suck the milk of nations,
    you will suck the wealth of kings,
and you will know that I,
    Yahweh, am your Saviour,
that your redeemer

is the Mighty One of Jacob.
¹⁷ For bronze I shall bring gold
and for iron I shall bring silver,
and for wood, bronze,
and for stone, iron;
I shall make Peace your administration
and Saving Justice your government.
¹⁸ Violence will no longer be heard of
in your country,
nor devastation and ruin
within your frontiers.
You will call your walls 'Salvation'
and your gates 'Praise'.

¹⁹ No more will the sun give you daylight,
nor moonlight shine on you,
but Yahweh will be your everlasting light,
your God will be your splendour.
²⁰ Your sun will set no more
nor will your moon wane,
for Yahweh will be your everlasting light
and your days of mourning will be over.
²¹ Your people, all of them upright,
will possess the country for ever,
the shoot I myself have planted,
my handiwork, for my own glory.
²² The smallest will grow into a thousand,
the weakest one into a mighty nation.

When the time is ripe, I, Yahweh,
shall quickly bring it about.

A PROPHET'S MISSION

61 The spirit of Lord Yahweh
is on me
for Yahweh has anointed me.
He has sent me to bring the news
     to the afflicted,
to soothe the broken-hearted,
2 to proclaim liberty to captives,
release to those in prison,
to proclaim a year of favour from Yahweh
and a day of vengeance for our God,
to comfort all who mourn
3 (to give to Zion's mourners),
to give them for ashes a garland,
for mourning-dress, the oil of gladness,
for despondency, festal attire;
and they will be called
     'terebinths of saving justice',
planted by Yahweh to glorify him.
4 They will rebuild the ancient ruins,
they will raise what has long lain waste,
they will restore the ruined cities,
all that has lain waste for ages past.
5 Strangers will come forward

to feed your flocks,
foreigners be your ploughmen
and vinedressers;

6 but you will be called 'priests of Yahweh'
and be addressed as 'ministers of our God'.
You will feed on the wealth of nations,
you will supplant them in their glory.

7 To make up for your shame,
you will receive double;
instead of disgrace,
shouts of joy will be their lot;
yes, they will have a double portion
in their country
and everlasting joy will be theirs.

8 For I am Yahweh: I love fair judgement,
I hate robbery and wrong-doing,
and I shall reward them faithfully
and make an everlasting covenant
with them.

9 Their race will be famous
throughout the nations
and their offspring
throughout the peoples.
All who see them will admit
that they are a race
whom Yahweh has blessed.

THANKSGIVING

¹⁰ I exult for joy in Yahweh,
    my soul rejoices in my God,
    for he has clothed me
        in garments of salvation,
    he has wrapped me in a cloak
        of saving justice,
    like a bridegroom wearing his garland,
    like a bride adorned in her jewels.
¹¹ For as the earth sends up its shoots
    and a garden makes seeds sprout,
    so Lord Yahweh makes saving justice
        and praise
spring up in the sight of all nations.

THE SPLENDOUR OF JERUSALEM

62 About Zion I will not be silent,
    about Jerusalem I shall not rest
until saving justice dawns for her
    like a bright light
and her salvation like a blazing torch.
² The nations will then see
    your saving justice,
    and all kings your glory,
    and you will be called a new name
    which Yahweh's mouth will reveal.

³ You will be a crown of splendour
    in Yahweh's hand,
a princely diadem in the hand of your God.
⁴ No more will you be known as 'Forsaken'
or your country be known as 'Desolation';
instead, you will be called
    'My Delight is in her'
and your country 'The Wedded';
for Yahweh will take delight in you
and your country will have its wedding.
⁵ Like a young man marrying a virgin,
your rebuilder will wed you,
and as the bridegroom rejoices in his bride,
so will your God rejoice in you.

⁶ On your walls, Jerusalem,
    I have posted watchmen;
they will never fall silent, day or night.
No peace for you,
    as you keep Yahweh's attention!
⁷ And give him no peace either
until he restores Jerusalem
and makes her the pride of the world!
⁸ Yahweh has sworn by his right hand
and by his mighty arm:
Never again shall I give your grain
to feed your enemies.
Never again will foreigners drink the wine

for which you have toiled.
9 No, the reapers will eat it
and praise Yahweh,
the harvesters will drink it
in my sacred courts!

CONCLUSION

10 Pass through, pass through the gates.
Clear a way for my people!
Level up, level up the highway,
remove the stones!
Hoist a signal to the peoples!
11 This is what Yahweh has proclaimed
to the remotest part of earth:
Say to the daughter of Zion,
'Look, your salvation is coming;
with him comes his reward,
his achievement precedes him!'

12 They will be called 'The Holy People',
'Yahweh's Redeemed',
while you will be called 'Sought-after',
'City-not-forsaken'.

JUDGEMENT OF THE NATIONS

63 Who is this coming from Edom,
from Bozrah in crimson garments,
so magnificently dressed,
marching so full of strength?
—It is I, whose word is saving justice,
whose power is to save.

2 —Why are your garments red,
your clothes like someone
treading the winepress?

3 —I have trodden the winepress alone;
of my people, not one was with me.
So I trod them down in my anger,
I trampled on them in my wrath.
Their blood squirted over my garments
and all my clothes are stained.

4 For I have decided on a day of vengeance,
my year of retribution has come.

5 I looked: there was no one to help me;
I was appalled but could find no supporter!
Then my own arm came to my rescue
and my own fury supported me.

6 I crushed the peoples in my anger,
I shattered them in my fury
and sent their blood streaming
to the ground.

MEDITATION ON THE HISTORY OF ISRAEL

7 I shall recount Yahweh's acts
    of faithful love,
Yahweh's praises,
in return for all
    that Yahweh has done for us,
for his great kindness
    to the House of Israel,
for all that he has done in his mercy,
for the abundance of his acts
    of faithful love.

8 For he said, 'Truly they are my people,
children who will not betray me,'
and he became their Saviour.
9 In all their troubles,
it was no messenger or angel
but his presence that saved them.
In his love and pity
he himself redeemed them,
lifted them up and carried them
throughout the days of old.
10 But they rebelled
and vexed his holy Spirit.
Then he became their enemy
and himself waged war on them.

¹¹ But he called the past to mind,
    Moses his servant.
    Where is he who saved them
        from the sea,
    the Shepherd of his flock?
    Where was he who put
    his holy Spirit among them,
¹² whose glorious arm led the way
    by Moses' right hand?
    Who divided the waters before them
    to win himself everlasting renown,
¹³ who led them through the depths
    as easily as a horse through the desert?
    They stumbled as little
¹⁴ as cattle going down to the plain.
    Yahweh's Spirit led them to rest.
    This was how you guided your people
    to win yourself glorious renown.

¹⁵ Look down from heaven and see
    from your holy and glorious dwelling.
    Where is your zeal and your might?
    Are your deepest feelings,
    your mercy to me, to be restrained?
¹⁶ After all, you are our Father.
    If Abraham will not own us,
    if Israel will not acknowledge us,
    you, Yahweh, are our Father,

'Our Redeemer' is your name from of old.

¹⁷ Why, Yahweh, do you let us wander
    from your ways
and let our hearts grow too hard
    to fear you?
Return, for the sake of your servants,
the tribes of your heritage.

¹⁸ Your holy people have owned it
    for so short a time,
our enemies have trampled
    on your sanctuary.

¹⁹ We have long been like those
    you do not rule,
people who do not bear your name.

Oh, that you would tear the heavens open
    and come down
—in your presence the mountains would quake,

64 as fire sets brushwood alight,
as fire makes water boil—
to make your name known to your foes;
the nations would tremble
    at your presence,

² at the unexpected miracles you would do.
(Oh, that you would come down,
in your presence
    the mountains would quake!)

³ Never has anyone heard,

no ear has heard, no eye has seen
any god but you act like this
for the sake of those who trust him.

4 You come to meet those
who are happy to act uprightly;
keeping your ways reminds them of you.
Yes, you have been angry
    and we have been sinners;
now we persist in your ways
    and we shall be saved.

5 We have all been like unclean things
and our upright deeds like filthy rags.
We wither, all of us, like leaves,
and all our misdeeds
    carry us off like the wind.

6 There is no one to invoke your name,
to rouse himself to hold fast to you,
for you have hidden your face from us
and given us up
    to the power of our misdeeds.

7 And yet, Yahweh, you are our Father;
we the clay and you our potter,
all of us are the work of your hands.

8 Yahweh, do not let your anger go too far
and do not remember guilt for ever.
Look, please, we are all your people;

9 your holy cities have become a desert,
Zion has become a desert,

Jerusalem a wasteland.

10 Our holy and glorious Temple,
in which our ancestors used to praise you,
has been burnt to the ground;
all our delight lies in ruins.

11 Yahweh, can you restrain yourself
at all this?
Will you stay
silentand afflict us beyond endurance?

THE COMING JUDGEMENT

65 I have let myself be approached
by those who did not consult me,
I have let myself be found
by those who did not seek me.
I said, 'Here I am, here I am!'
to a nation that did not invoke my name.

2 Each day I stretched out my hands
to a rebellious people
who follow a way which is not good,
as the fancy takes them;

3 a people constantly provoking me
to my face
by sacrificing in gardens,
burning incense on bricks,

4 living in tombs,
spending the night in dark corners,

eating the meat of pigs,
putting unclean foods on their plates.
5   'Keep your distance,' they say,
'do not touch me,
     lest my sanctity come near you!'
Such words are like stifling smoke to me,
an ever-burning fire.
6   Look, it is inscribed before me:
I shall not be silent
     until I have repaid them,
repaid them in full,
7   punished your guilt
     and your ancestors' guilt together,
Yahweh declares.
For having burnt incense on the mountains
and insulted me on the hills,
I shall pay them back in full
     for what they have done.

8   Yahweh says this:
As when a bunch of grapes is found
     still to have juice in it,
people say, 'Do not destroy it,
for it contains a blessing,'
so I shall act for my servants' sake,
I shall not destroy them all.
9   I shall produce descendants from Jacob
and heirs to my mountains from Judah,

my chosen ones will own them
and my servants will live there.

¹⁰ Sharon will be a pasture for flocks,
the Valley of Achor
a feeding ground for cattle,
for those of my people
who have sought me.

¹¹ But as for those of you
who abandon Yahweh,
who forget my holy mountain,
who lay the table for Gad,²⁵
who fill cups of mixed wine for Meni,

¹² you I shall destine to the sword
and all of you will stoop to be slaughtered,
because I called and you would not answer,
I spoke and you would not listen;
you have done what I consider evil,
you chose to do what displeases me.

¹³ Therefore Lord Yahweh says this:
You will see my servants eating
while you go hungry;
you will see my servants drinking
while you go thirsty;
you will see my servants rejoicing
while you are put to shame;

¹⁴ you will hear my servants
shouting for joy of heart,
while you shriek for sorrow of heart

and howl with a broken spirit.

15 And you will leave your name behind
   as a curse for my chosen ones,
'May Lord Yahweh strike you dead!'
But to his servants
   he will give another name.

16 Whoever blesses himself on earth
   will bless himself by the God of truth,
and whoever swears an oath on earth
   will swear by the God of truth,
for past troubles will be forgotten
and hidden from my eyes.

17 For look, I am going to create
   new heavens and a new earth,
and the past will not be remembered
and will come no more to mind.

18 Rather be joyful, be glad for ever
at what I am creating,
   for look, I am creating Jerusalem
      to be 'Joy'
and my people to be 'Gladness'.

19 I shall be joyful in Jerusalem
and I shall rejoice in my people.
No more will the sound of weeping
   be heard there,
nor the sound of a shriek;

20 never again will there be an infant there
   who lives only a few days,

nor an old man who does not run
    his full course;
for the youngest will die at a hundred,
and at a hundred
    the sinner will be accursed.
21 They will build houses and live in them,
    they will plant vineyards and eat their fruit.
22 They will not build for others to live in,
    or plant for others to eat;
for the days of my people
    will be like the days of a tree,
and my chosen ones will themselves use
    what they have made.
23 They will not toil in vain,
    nor bear children destined to disaster,
for they are the race
    of Yahweh's blessed ones
and so are their offspring.
24 Thus, before they call I shall answer,
    before they stop speaking
        I shall have heard.
25 The wolf and the young lamb
    will feed together,
the lion will eat hay like the ox,
and dust be the serpent's food.
No hurt, no harm will be done
on all my holy mountain,
    Yahweh says.

PROPHECY ON THE TEMPLE

66 Thus says Yahweh:
With heaven my throne
and earth my footstool,
what house could you build me,
what place for me to rest,

2 when all these things were made by me
and all belong to me?—declares Yahweh.
But my eyes are drawn to the person
of humbled and contrite spirit,
who trembles at my word.

3 Some slaughter a bull,
some kill a human being,
some sacrifice a lamb, some strangle a dog,
some present an offering of pig's blood,
some burn memorial incense,
a revolting blessing;
all these people have chosen
their own ways
and take delight
in their disgusting practices.

4 I too take delight in making fools of them,
I shall bring what they most fear
down on them
because I have called
and no one would answer,

I spoke and no one listened.
They have done what I regard as evil,
have chosen what displeases me.

JUDGEMENT ON JERUSALEM

5 Listen to the word of Yahweh,
  you who tremble at his word.
  Your brothers, who hate and reject you
  because of my name, have said,
  'Let Yahweh show his glory,
  let us witness your joy!'
  But they will be put to shame.

6 Listen! An uproar from the city!
  A voice from the Temple!
  The voice of Yahweh
  bringing retribution on his enemies.

7 Before being in labour
    she has given birth.
  Before the birth pangs came,
    she has been delivered of a child.

8 Who ever heard of such a thing,
  who ever saw anything like this?
  Can a country be born in one day?
  Can a nation be brought forth

all at once?
For Zion, scarcely in labour,
    has brought forth her children!

9 Shall I open the womb
    and not bring to birth?
says Yahweh.
Shall I, who bring to birth,
    close the womb?
says your God.

10 Rejoice with Jerusalem,
be glad for her, all you who love her!
Rejoice, rejoice with her,
all you who mourned her!

11 So that you may be suckled and satisfied
from her consoling breast,
so that you may drink deep with
from her generous nipple.

12 For Yahweh says this:
Look, I am going to send peace
flowing over her like a river,
and like a stream in spate
the glory of the nations.

You will be suckled, carried on her hip
and fondled in her lap.
13 As a mother comforts a child,
    so I shall comfort you;
    you will be comforted in Jerusalem.

14 At the sight your heart will rejoice,
    and your limbs regain
        like the grass.
    To his servants
        Yahweh will reveal his hand,
    but to his enemies his fury.

15 For see how Yahweh comes in fire
    his chariots like the whirlwind,
    to assuage his anger with burning,
    his rebukes with flaming fire.

16 For by fire will Yahweh execute
        fair judgement,
    and by his sword, on all people;
    and Yahweh's victims will be many.
17 As for those who sanctify themselves
    and purify themselves
        to enter the gardens,
    following the one in the centre,
    who eat the flesh of pigs,
        revolting things and rats:

their deeds and their thoughts
will perish together,
declares Yahweh.

AN ESCHATOLOGICAL DISCOURSE

[18]I am coming to gather every nation and every language.
They will come to witness my glory. [19]I shall give them a
sign and send some of their survivors to the nations: to
Tarshish, Put, Lud, Meshech, Tubal and Javan,[a] to the distant
coasts and islands that have never heard of me or seen my
glory. They will proclaim my glory to the nations, [20]and
from all the nations they will bring all your brothers as an
offering to Yahweh, on horses, in chariots, in litters, on
mules and on camels, to my holy mountain, Jerusalem,
Yahweh says, like Israelites bringing offerings in clean
vessels to Yahweh's house. [21]And some of them I shall make
into priests and Levites, Yahweh says.

[22]For as the new heavens and the new earth I am
making will endure before me, declares Yahweh, so will
your race and your name endure.

[23] From New Moon
to New Moon, from Sabbath
to Sabbath, all humanity will come and bow
in my presence, Yahweh says.
[24] And on their way out they will see
the corpses of those

who rebelled against me;
for their worm will never die
nor their fire be put out,
and they will be held in horror
    by all humanity.